CORE FOCUS

GRADE 5

TEST PRACTICE
for Common Core

Sheila Frye, Ed.D.
Reading Specialist
Montville School District
Montville, NJ

and

Lisa M. Hall, M.Ed., NBCT
Title I Mathematics Specialist
Henrico County Public Schools
Richmond, VA

BARRON'S

About the Authors

Sheila Frye is an elementary reading specialist and a literacy innovation researcher. She holds a doctorate degree from Rutgers University in the Design of Learning Environments, where she researched the crossroads between interactive eBook applications and reading comprehension. Sheila has been in education for more than seventeen years and has certifications as a reading specialist, special education teacher, and supervisor. You can find her on Tumblr (teachingliteracy. tumblr.com), Twitter @sheila_frye, or email: sheila.frye@icloud.com.

Lisa Hall is the Title I Mathematics Specialist at Cashell Donahoe Elementary School in Henrico County, Virginia. She is a National Board Certified Teacher and a recipient of the Presidential Award for Excellence in Mathematics Teaching. She has 28 years of teaching experience at the elementary, middle, and college levels. Lisa gives numerous presentations at state and national math conferences, where she shares techniques and strategies that have helped her at-risk students experience success.

All inquiries should be addressed to:
Barron's Educational Series, Inc.
250 Wireless Boulevard
Hauppauge, New York 11788
www.barronseduc.com

ISBN: 978-1-4380-0595-9

Library of Congress Control Number: 2014950751

Manufactured by: B11R11
Date of Manufacture: March 2015

PRINTED IN THE UNITED STATES OF AMERICA
9 8 7 6 5 4 3 2

CONTENTS

ENGLISH LANGUAGE ARTS

Language

Reading: Literature

Reading: Informational Text

Writing

MATH

Operations and Algebraic Thinking

Number and Operations in Base 10

Number and Operations—Fractions

Measurement and Data

Geometry

NOTE TO PARENTS AND EDUCATORS

About Barron's Core Focus Workbooks

Barron's recognizes the need to create a product that will help students navigate the Common Core State Standards being implemented in many schools across America. To meet this need, we have created grade-specific workbooks that will help bring the Common Core standards to life and ensure that students are prepared for these recently implemented national assessments and expectations in learning. It is our hope that students can work through these books independently or with the guidance of a parent or teacher.

Barron's Core Focus workbooks are meant to supplement the Common Core teaching that students are receiving in their classrooms or other learning environment. These workbooks, all created by dedicated educators, provide specific practice on the Common Core standards through a variety of exercises and question types, including multiple-choice, short-answer, and extended-response. The questions are organized to build on each other, increasing student understanding from one standard to the next, one step at a time, and they challenge students to apply the standards in different formats. Both the English Language Arts (ELA) and Math sections of the books end with a review test—this is a great way to sum up what the student has learned and reviewed from the exercises throughout.

What Is the Common Core?

"The standards are designed to be robust and relevant to the real world, reflecting the knowledge and skills that our young people need for success in college and careers."

(2012 Common Core State Standards Initiative)

Simply put, the Common Core is a series of standards that spell out exactly what students are expected to learn in English Language Arts and Mathematics throughout their years in school. These standards are fairly consistent across all grades and are designed so that students, teachers, and parents can understand what students should be learning and achieving at each grade level. Standards are organized to provide a clear understanding of the core concepts and procedures that students should master at each step of the way through school.

Unlike previous standards that were created by individual states, the Common Core is meant to be consistent throughout the country, providing all students with an equal and fair opportunity to learn English Language Arts (ELA) and Math. These standards are also designed to teach students how to apply this knowledge to their everyday lives and experiences.

By sharing the same standards, states can more accurately gauge and compare students' progress and the quality of education received. The ultimate goal of Common Core is to ensure that all students, no matter which state or part of the country they are from, will be equally ready and prepared for college and the workforce.

What Is a Standard?

A standard is a skill that should be learned by a student. Standards are organized by *domains*, which are larger groupings of related standards. For instance, in grade 5 math, there are five domains, including: Operation and Algebraic Thinking, Number and Operations in Base Ten, and Measurement and Data.

Under the domain Number and Operations: Fractions, there are seven standards. These standards highlight the specific skill or understanding that a student should gain. One standard, **NF.B.4**, directs students to "apply and extend previous understandings of multiplication to multiply a fraction or whole number by a fraction." For example, by knowing that 6 multiplied by 5 means 6 groups of 5, a student will also know that 6 multiplied by 1/5 means 6 groups of 1/5.

ENGLISH LANGUAGE ARTS

The English Language Arts standards are separated into different strands. The K–5 standards are comprehensive and are divided into the following areas: Reading, Writing, Speaking and Listening, Foundational Skills, and Language. The Common Core has designated separate reading standards for both fiction and nonfiction texts. These standards are identified as Reading: Literature, and Reading: Informational Text. Most important, the reading standards emphasize engaging all students in the reading process. To meet the standards, students are expected to read multiple forms of texts, which will provide deeper literary experiences for all students. The Common Core also emphasizes the importance of text complexity. "Through extensive reading of stories, dramas, poems, and myths from diverse cultures and different time periods, students gain literary and cultural knowledge as well as familiarity with various text structures and elements." (2012 Common Core State Standards Initiative)

Each of the K–5 strands is arranged within a College and Career Readiness Anchor Standard. The Anchor Standards are the overarching goals of a K–12 curriculum. These standards remain constant in all grades. Each grade level's strands are built as scaffolds in order to achieve "official" College and Career Readiness Anchor Standards by the end of the twelfth grade. The College and Career Readiness Anchor Standards for Reading Literature and Informational Text focus on identifying key ideas and details, craft and structure, and the integration of knowledge and ideas. To meet the Common Core reading standards, students are expected to read, respond to, and interact with an array of text types of varying complexities. The College and Career Readiness Anchor Standards for Writing focus on text types and purposes, production and distribution of writing, and research to build and present knowledge. To meet the Common Core writing standards, students are expected to write persuasive, narrative, and informational text. The College and Career Readiness Anchor Standards for Speaking and Listening focus on comprehension, collaboration, and presentation of knowledge and ideas. The speaking and listening standards focus heavily on students' ability to actively participate in groups, engage with others, and present academic information in multiple settings. The College and Career Readiness Anchor Standards for Language focus on the conventions of standard English, vocabulary acquisition, and knowledge of language.

The Common Core standards are also designed to help students create digital literature and use technology to communicate ideas and knowledge. The English Language Arts standards are a vision of what it means to be literate in the twenty-first century. These standards foster imperative learning experiences for the twenty-first century learner. "The skills and knowledge captured in the ELA/literacy standards are designed to prepare students for life outside the classroom. They include critical-thinking skills and the ability to closely and attentively read texts in a way that will help them understand and enjoy complex works of literature." (2012 Common Core State Standards Initiative)

MATH

The Common Core mathematics standards were developed as a connected progression of learning throughout grades K–12. Ideally, this will enable teachers to close achievement gaps and give students the foundational skills necessary to continue in their learning. The Common Core provides teachers with an opportunity to build a deep and rich understanding of mathematical concepts. Instruction of Common Core mathematics standards encompasses the Mathematical Practices as well. These practices include skills that math students in every grade are expected to master. The Mathematical Practices bring rigor and rich learning opportunities to the classroom.

In grade 5, Operations and Algebraic Thinking is a challenging domain that is taught to students. In grade 4, students learned to generate single number patterns based on a single rule. In grade 5, students are now expected to generate two numerical patterns using two given rules. The Common Core standards are related across grade levels as well as across the domains. For example, Measurement and Data standards share a relationship with Operations and Algebraic Thinking standards. This connectedness helps students prepare for the real world—remember, we do not use just one skill to balance our checkbook or determine the amount of paint for a room in our home. We have to apply a variety of skills every day, and a goal of the Common Core math standards is to help prepare students for this real-life use of math. The Common Core also supports mathematical understanding of concepts that are developmentally appropriate for students. These standards allow students to build strong number sense in the early grades as they learn to count, to order numbers, and to compare numbers to help them think about numbers flexibly and to understand the relationships between numbers as they move into the higher grades.

HOW TO USE THIS BOOK

This test practice workbook is organized by standard—one step at a time—in the order students will likely see the concepts in the classroom or other learning environment. Each applicable standard is organized in an easy-to-navigate spread(s), providing exposure to the Common Core in the simplest way possible. This format is consistent throughout the Math section of the workbook; however, because of the nature of the ELA curriculum, standards that share a common goal may be grouped together in spreads throughout this section of the workbook (see pages 12–13).

In these workbooks, students will be able to build skills in multiple formats by answering multiple-choice, short-answer, and extended-response questions. Answers and explanations are included at the end of each section so students, parents, and teachers can easily assess the student's response. These explanations are an important part of the learning process as they provide information on the understanding needed to answer each question, common misconceptions students may have, and an explanation of how students might best approach and respond to the question. These explanations will help students not only check the accuracy of their responses but also learn how they can improve their responses. Students using **Barron's Core Focus** workbooks will practice each of the specific content standards as they learn them, and also thoroughly review all the concepts in Math or English Language Arts through the cumulative assessments.

> A complete list of the English Language Arts and Math Common Core Standards can be found in the back of this book in Appendices A and B.

In addition to the practice spreads covering specific standards, each section ends with a comprehensive practice test that allows students to monitor their general progress in either English Language Arts or Math. Answers and explanations provide additional guidance and instruction.

FEATURES AND BENEFITS

Barron's Core Focus workbooks provide educators, parents, and students with the opportunity to enhance their knowledge and to practice grade-level expectations within the Common Core English Language Arts and Math standards. Each workbook in this series provides questions that correlate to each standard. Every answer explanation provides insight into a student's understanding, identifying common misconceptions and providing multiple strategies. Each book also provides a cumulative assessment for each content area in Math and English Language Arts. Throughout the books, there are "Fast Fact" boxes that contain a variety of information and expose students to vocabulary, tips, and strategies.

- Parents can use these books to encourage learning at home. They can be used as guided practice or extra exposure to concepts students may be struggling to master in school.

- Educators can use the workbooks in their classrooms to identify how to assess each standard. These books give teachers insight into what students should be able to do independently in order to master the standard. The detailed answer explanations provide opportunities for teachers to recognize misconceptions students may have about specific standards and how to successfully approach questions applicable to each standard.

- Students can use these workbooks at home to build their knowledge of English Language Arts and Math content. They can practice the content they have learned, are learning, or are going to learn. The workbooks can be used to help prepare students for what's to come and/or as remedial practice for concepts that they find challenging. The explanations in the books are extremely valuable to students as they work independently, increasing their awareness of concepts and improving their confidence as they work through each question.

The benefits that **Barron's Core Focus** workbooks will provide students, parents, and teachers are endless as the Common Core is implemented in schools across America.

Common Core State Standards Initiative
http://www.corestandards.org/

PARCC
http://www.parcconline.org/

Smarter Balance Assessment Consortium
www.smarterbalanced.org

ENGLISH LANGUAGE ARTS

The English Language Arts Standards are separated into different strands. The K–5 standards are comprehensive and are divided into the following areas: Reading, Writing, Speaking and Listening, Foundational Skills, and Language. The Common Core has designated separate reading standards for both fiction and nonfiction texts. These standards are identified as Reading: Literature and Reading: Informational Text. In this section, students will practice skills covering a variety of standards. Each section covers a specific standard covered in grade 5 and provides the student with practice through multiple-choice, short-answer, and extended-response questions.

CONJUNCTIONS, PREPOSITIONS, AND INTERJECTIONS

Directions: Circle the appropriate conjunction to be used in each sentence.

1. Deepa would love to go on the roller coaster (but/so) she is afraid of heights.

2. Marvin can cook pasta (nor/or) he can just eat the leftovers from yesterday.

> Prepositions show the position or direction of one word to another.

3. Tricia is good at soccer (for/yet) her favorite sport is dance.

Directions: Circle the appropriate correlative conjunctions to be used in each sentence.

4. (Either/Both) Emily (and/nor) Saahil went to camp last summer.

5. (Neither/Either) do your chores (and/or) you will not get an allowance.

6. (Not/Neither) my uncle (nor/or) my grandmother can go to the movies with us.

Directions: Circle the preposition(s) in each sentence.

7. Tanny took a walk around the park with her dog.

8. The marker fell between the table and the wall.

9. Alton looked under the bed for his missing book.

Directions: Write a sentence using each interjection given below.

Ex: (Hey) *Hey, you can't sleep on the couch all day!*

10. (Whoa)

_____

_____

11. (Oops)

_____

_____

12. (Woohoo)

_____

_____

(Answers are on page 59.)

VERB TENSES

L.5.1 Demonstrate command of the conventions of standard English grammar and usage when writing or speaking.
L.5.1.B Form and use the perfect (e.g., I had walked; I have walked; I will have walked) verb tenses.
L.5.1.C Use verb tense to convey various times, sequences, states, and conditions.
L.5.1.D Recognize and correct inappropriate shifts in verb tense.

Directions: Circle the appropriate perfect verb tense to be used in each sentence.

1. By next winter, Kai (have completed/had completed/will have completed) all of the practice sessions.

2. The train (has arrived/had arrived/will have arrived) and is now filling up with new passengers.

3. Sasha could not remember if she (has locked/had locked/will have locked) the front door earlier, so she went back to check.

> Verbs are action words. The perfect tense of a verb describes an action that has, was, or will have been completed. You have to use the "to have" verb + the past participle of the verb.

Directions: Circle the verb. Then write if the verb in each sentence is in the present, past, or future tense.

4. Jack carefully spreads the peanut butter on the bread.

   present tense

5. The bus will leave at 3:00 pm on Friday.

   future tense

6. Milan and his sister walked to the beach in the morning.

   past tense

Directions: Rewrite the following sentences replacing the underlined word(s) with the verb in the appropriate tense.

7. Every time Aaliyah scored a goal, her team <u>will yell</u> loudly.

   future _____

8. The parents will travel by car and the kids <u>travels</u> by bus.

   _____

9. All of the chimpanzees gather in the jungle and <u>searched</u> for ants.

   _____

10. Jaden cleaned his room and <u>stacks</u> his books in a neat pile.

   _____

(Answers are on page 59.)

CAPITALIZATION, PUNCTUATION, AND SPELLING

L.5.2 Demonstrate command of the conventions of standard English capitalization, punctuation, and spelling when writing.
L.5.2.A Use punctuation to separate items in a series.
L.5.2.B Use a comma to separate an introductory element from the rest of the sentence.
L.5.2.C Use a comma to set off the words yes and no (e.g., Yes, thank you), to set off a tag question from the rest of the sentence (e.g., It's true, isn't it?), and to indicate direct address (e.g., Is that you, Steve?).

Directions: Darken the letter of the sentence that has NO errors in punctuation or capitalization.

1. Ⓐ the first World cup tournament took place in 1930 in montevideo, Uruguay.
   Ⓑ The first world cup tournament took place in 1930 in montevideo, uruguay
   Ⓒ The first World Cup tournament took place in 1930 in Montevideo, Uruguay.
   Ⓓ The first world Cup tournament took place in 1930 in Montevideo, Uruguay

2. Ⓐ Amelia Earhart was the first female pilot to fly solo across the Atlantic Ocean.
   Ⓑ amelia Earhart was the first female pilot to fly solo across the atlantic ocean.
   Ⓒ Amelia Earhart was the first female pilot to fly solo across the Atlantic ocean.
   Ⓓ amelia earhart was the first female pilot to fly solo across the Atlantic ocean

Directions: Finish each sentence by filling in the correctly spelled word.

3. Arin's _____ ice cream flavor is chocolate chip cookie dough.
   Ⓐ favorete
   Ⓑ faverite
   Ⓒ favorite

4. After agreeing to go to the movies with his friend, Ibrahim had to _____ which movie they would see.
   Ⓐ deturmin
   Ⓑ determine
   Ⓒ deetermun

6

Directions: Read each sentence. Add commas where necessary to create a grammatically correct sentence.

5. Maya Angelou was a famous African-American poet author dancer singer and actress.

6. Yes I would love to go to the concert with you on Friday!

7. If you don't study you will not be ready for the social studies quiz.

8. We had pizza cookies and cake at Noah's 11th birthday party.

9. Freddy I never knew you could jump so high!

10. Come to think of it I do want to visit the museum in New York City.

(Answers are on page 60.)

UNDERSTANDING VOCABULARY

> **L.5.4** Determine or clarify the meaning of unknown and multiple-meaning words and phrases based on grade 5 reading and content, choosing flexibly from a range of strategies.
> **L.5.4.A** Use context (e.g., cause/effect relationships and comparisons in text) as a clue to the meaning of a word or phrase.
> **L.5.4.B** Use common, grade-appropriate Greek and Latin affixes and roots as clues to the meaning of a word (e.g., photograph, photosynthesis).

Directions: Read the sentence and select the best definition for the word in bold. Underline the context clues (words or phrases) that helped you determine the word's meaning.

1. The water was so **frigid** that it made Akiko shiver.

   Frigid most likely means
   - Ⓐ shallow
   - Ⓑ cold
   - Ⓒ hot
   - Ⓓ deep

2. Both candidates **vied** for the position of class president and put up posters around the entire school.
   Vied most likely means
   - Ⓐ competed
   - Ⓑ showed
   - Ⓒ traded
   - Ⓓ avoided

3. The new video game had such **favorable** reviews that it sold out in just one day.

   Favorable most likely means _____

4. Ezra did not understand what he was supposed to do, so he asked his teacher to **clarify** the directions.

   Clarify most likely means _____

8

Directions: Use your knowledge of common Greek and Latin affixes and roots to help determine the meaning of the words in bold.

5. After Max cleaned the window, it was more **transparent** than ever before. What is the meaning of the affix, **trans-**?
   Ⓐ through
   Ⓑ build
   Ⓒ best

6. **Transparent** most likely means
   Ⓐ able to be created
   Ⓑ able to go from one place to another
   Ⓒ able to be better than before
   Ⓓ able to see through

7. Isabella's mother is a **geologist** who studies rocks from different canyons. What is the meaning of the root word, **geo-**?
   Ⓐ shape
   Ⓑ birth
   Ⓒ earth

8. **Geologist** most likely means
   Ⓐ a person who studies different shapes
   Ⓑ a person who studies water animals
   Ⓒ a person who studies the earth's surface
   Ⓓ a person who studies plants

9. The local **aquifer** was full after a season of heavy rains. What is the meaning of the root word, **aqu-**?
   Ⓐ land
   Ⓑ water
   Ⓒ star

10. **Aquifer** most likely means
    Ⓐ an underground area that holds water
    Ⓑ the bumpy land around a jungle or forest
    Ⓒ a place where stars collect
    Ⓓ a machine used to measure storms

(Answers are on page 60.)

FIGURATIVE LANGUAGE

L.5.5 Demonstrate understanding of figurative language, word relationships, and nuances in word meanings.
L.5.5.A Interpret figurative language, including similes and metaphors, in context.
L.5.5.B Recognize and explain the meaning of common idioms, adages, and proverbs.
L.5.5.C Use the relationship between particular words (e.g., synonyms, antonyms, homographs) to better understand each of the words.

Directions: Read each sentence and determine if a simile or metaphor is being used. Then explain the meaning of the simile or metaphor.

1. The mystery was a puzzle that needed to be solved.
   - (A) simile
   - (B) metaphor

   Explain the meaning of the expression.

   _____

2. My backpack is so full that it is as heavy as an elephant.
   - (A) simile
   - (B) metaphor

   Explain the meaning of the expression.

   _____

3. Leonardo is the shining star of our class because he works hard and treats people with respect.
   - (A) simile
   - (B) metaphor

   Explain the meaning of the expression.

   _____

Directions: Explain the meaning of the idiom, adage, or proverb used in each sentence.

4. Nina's grandmother believes that **every cloud has a silver lining**.

   Explain the meaning of the expression.

   _____

   _____

5. Zora does not always **see eye to eye** with Abby.

Explain the meaning of the expression.

_____

_____

6. Ryan and Angelo have been friends **through thick and thin**.

Explain the meaning of the expression.

_____

_____

Directions: Read each sentence to find the meaning of the underlined word. Use the word in italics as a clue.

7. Stefan is very *popular* but his sister is more <u>withdrawn</u> and prefers to be alone.

<u>Withdrawn</u> most likely means
- Ⓐ loud
- Ⓑ private
- Ⓒ happy
- Ⓓ outgoing

8. Once I *finish* this level, I will <u>progress</u> to the championship round.

<u>Progress</u> most likely means
- Ⓐ develop
- Ⓑ grow
- Ⓒ jump
- Ⓓ move

9. Instead of a *smile*, Esperanza had a huge <u>grimace</u> on her face when she heard that she had to finish her chores.

<u>Grimace</u> most likely means
- Ⓐ scowl
- Ⓑ grin
- Ⓒ mark
- Ⓓ smirk

10. The flowers are so <u>fragrant</u> that I stop to *smell* them every day.

<u>Fragrant</u> most likely means
- Ⓐ stinky
- Ⓑ bright
- Ⓒ sweetly scented
- Ⓓ large

(Answers are on page 60.)

MAKE INFERENCES AND DETERMINE WORD MEANING

RL.5.1 Quote accurately from a text when explaining what the text says explicitly and when drawing inferences from the text.
RL.5.4 Determine the meaning of words and phrases as they are used in a text, including figurative language such as metaphors and similes.

Directions: Read the following passage from *Solomon Snow and the Silver Spoon* by Kate Umansky. Then answer the following questions about the passage.

Solomon Snow was walking along a quiet country lane, minding his own business thinking vague thoughts, when a voice spoke in his ear, almost making him jump out of his boots.

"Where are you going, boy?" said the voice.

Solly looked up. Poking down at him from between the leaves of a chestnut tree was a nose.

Uh-oh. His heart sank. He knew that nose. It was attached to that weird Prudence Pridy from the village. Eldest daughter of the local poacher, who was currently in jail. (Again.) Usually had her unfortunate appendage buried in a book, because the village boys sang a rude song about it. Not that he'd ever joined in, of course.

What did she want with him?

Right now, she was perched on a branch, skinny legs dangling, an open composition book in her lap. A gnawed pencil stuck out of her ugly straw bonnet in a mad sort of way.

"What are you doing up there?" asked Solly rather gruffly. He wasn't used to talking to girls.

"Sitting," said Prudence.

"Oh. Right." He would have left it at that and continued on his way, but it wasn't meant to be.

"What's in your bundle?" demanded Prudence.

"Dirty washing," said Solly with a sigh. "Old Mother Rust's winter unmentionables."

He glanced at his bundle. Old Mother Rust's winter unmentionables only got washed once a year. He would be glad to get them home. He had a feeling they might burst into flames.

"Got anything to eat?"

Ah. Right. That's why she was talking to him.

"Well, just a bit of crust I'm saving for my dinner—"

"Stand back," ordered Prudence, stuffing her book into a handy hole in the trunk. "I'm coming down."

There was a flurry of brown and a shower of twigs and leaves. Seconds later, she stood before him, ankle deep in autumn leaves. Solly thrust his hand into his pocket, fingers closing protectively over his pathetically small hunk of bread.

Prudence Pridy was tall and gawky and seemed to be built from knees and elbows. Everything about her was all wrong. Her boots were too big and her hat was too horrible, even without the pencil sticking out. Her dress was a brown shapeless sack. As for the nose—well. You only had to look. It was long. It was pointed. It ruled her face. You couldn't stop staring at it.

"Shouldn't you be in class?" asked Solly. Prudence, he knew, attended the village charity school, where you got free meals. He had seen her marching through the gates at the head of a long line of small, squabbling sisters.

"I'm not going to school anymore," said Prudence.

"Oh? Why not?" He hoped if he got her talking, it might divert her mind to things other than the crust in his pocket. Besides, to tell the truth, he was curious. He had never been to school.

"Because I hate it, and the toilets smell." Prudence flicked her mousy braids and gave a haughty sniff. "Anyway, I know all I need to know. She can't teach me anything."

1. Read this sentence from the story:

   "Solly thrust his hand into his pocket, fingers closing protectively over his **pathetically** small hunk of bread."

   What is the meaning of the word **pathetically** as it is used in this sentence?
   Ⓐ decently
   Ⓑ usefully
   Ⓒ sadly
   Ⓓ gloriously

2. Which word from the sentence helps the reader understand the meaning of **pathetically**?

   _____

13

3. Which excerpt does the author include to help the reader understand Solly's feelings toward Prudence?

Ⓐ "Uh-oh. His heart sank."

Ⓑ "'Well, just a bit of crust I'm saving for my dinner —'"

Ⓒ "'What are you doing up there?' asked Solly rather gruffly. He wasn't used to talking to girls."

Ⓓ "Solomon Snow was walking along a quiet country lane, minding his own business thinking vague thoughts, when a voice spoke in his ear, almost making him jump out of his boots."

4. It can be inferred from the passage that Solly does not want to share his bread with Prudence. Provide evidence from the story to support this inference.

_____

_____

5. What does Solly mean when he thinks, "Ah. Right. That's why she was talking to him."?

Ⓐ Prudence is hoping to become friends with Solly.

Ⓑ Prudence is only talking to Solly because she is hungry.

Ⓒ Prudence is nosy and likes to know what other people are doing.

Ⓓ Prudence is bored and needs something fun to do.

6. Read this excerpt from the story:

"'Because I hate it, and the toilets smell.' Prudence flicked her mousy braids and gave a **haughty** sniff. 'Anyway, I know all I need to know. She can't teach me anything.'"

What is the meaning of the word **haughty** as it is used in the sentence?

Ⓐ loud

Ⓑ curious

Ⓒ light

Ⓓ snooty

7. Read this excerpt from the story:

   "As for the nose—well. You only had to look. It was long. It was pointed. **It ruled her face.**"

   What is meant by the phrase, "It ruled her face"?

   _____

   _____

   _____

8. It can be inferred from the passage that Solly is a good-hearted person. Provide evidence from the story to support this inference.

   _____

   _____

   _____

(Answers are on page 61.)

COMPARE AND CONTRAST PAIRED TEXTS

RL.5.3 Compare and contrast two or more characters, settings, or events in a story or drama, drawing on specific details in the text (e.g., how characters interact).
RL.5.9 Compare and contrast stories in the same genre (e.g., mysteries and adventure stories) on their approaches to similar themes and topics.

Directions: Read the following passages from *Rodzina* by Karen Cushman and *Ruby Holler* by Sharon Creech. Then answer the following questions about the passages.

Passage 1

Chicago, 1881

On a cold Monday morning in March, when a weak, pale sun struggled to shine and ice glistened in the cracks in the wooden street, a company of some twenty-two orphan children with stiff new clothes and little cardboard suitcases boarded a special railway car at the station near the Chicago River. I know, because I was one of them.

The station was noisier and more confused than Halsted Street on market day. Travelers carrying featherbeds and bundles wrapped in blue gingham cloth shoved me aside in their hurry to get here or there. A man in a bright red jacket bumped into me and apologized in a language I did not know. At least I assumed it was an apology, because of all the bowing and tipping of his hat, so I said, "It's all right, mister, but I'd say you should know a little English if you expect to get wherever you're going." He tipped his hat again.

One woman, burdened with children, blankets, a tin kettle, and a three-legged stove, finally put that stove right down on the platform, sat herself atop it, and began to cry. I knew how she felt. I myself was a mite worried—not scared, being twelve and no baby like Evelyn or Gertie to be afraid of every little thing, but worried, yes. It was all so loud and disorderly and unfamiliar.

I forced my way through the crowd and grabbed on to a belt in front of me. The boy it belonged to said, "Hang on tight, Rodzina, afore we're swept into the lake like sewage." It was Spud, whom I knew from the Little Wanderers' Refuge. He and Chester, Gertie, Horton, Rose and Pearl Lubnitz, the baby Evelyn, and I—we had been there together. The others were from the Infant Hospital and the Orphan Asylum near Hyde Park. Orphans, all of us, carrying all we owned in our two hands, pushing and shoving like everyone else.

A lady, standing straight and tall in a black suit and still white shirtwaist, put her hands up to her mouth and shouted, but I could not hear much over the din. I finally gathered that she was from the Orphan Asylum and was calling us all together. Letting go of Spud's belt, I stretched myself even taller so I could get a better look at her over that expanse of heads. She was pale and thin, her mouth ill-humored, and her gray eyes as cold and sharp as the wire rims of her spectacles. I should have known they would not send someone kind and good-natured to accompany a carload of orphans.

Roaring and cursing, a short, barrel-shaped man togged out in a checked jacket and yellow shoes pushed his way through the crowd. "You! Orphans!" he shouted, the cigar in the corner of his mouth waving and waggling with his words. "Pipe down! I am Mr. Szprot, the placing-out agent for the Association of Aid Societies. That means I am the boss and you do what I tell you."

Passage 2

The Boxton Creek Home

Boxton was a tired town, a neglected place that looked as if it was in danger of collapsing in on itself. A tangle of old homes and shacks clustered around small stores and buildings that had seen better days. One of these buildings was the Boxton Creek Home for Children, a ramshackle house that tilted toward the train tracks and hills beyond. In this building lived the bungling managers, Mr. and Mrs. Trepid; their assistant, Morgan; and thirteen children, ranging in age from six months to thirteen years.

The two oldest children in the Boxton Creek Home were twins, Dallas and Florida. They were tall for their age, dark-haired and dark-eyed, with sturdy frames and a rough-edged and unkempt look about them. Dallas was the quieter of the two and the one more included to daydreaming, while Florida was loud and squirmy, with her mouth full of words bursting out, and her face full of expression, flashing from surprise to disgust in an instant.

The managers of the Home, Mr. and Mrs. Trepid, were middle-aged, cranky and tired, and growing stiff and cold as winter-bound trees. They believed in rules, and their rules were posted on doorways and in hallways and above each child's bed. There were general rules and kitchen rules, bathroom rules and stairway rules, basement rules and outside rules, upstairs rules and downstairs rules, clothing rules, washing rules, cleaning rules, rules upon rules upon rules.

"If we didn't have rules," Mr. Trepid liked to say, "everything would be chaos."

"If we didn't have rules," his wife would say, "these children would eat us alive."

Since Dallas and Florida had lived in the Boxton Creek Home longer than any of the other children there, they knew all the rules. They also knew the punishments for disobeying the rules, and they knew them well, because they had broken every rule in the Boxton Creek Home. Many times.

"How can we live every day of our lives without running or shouting or throwing or talking or dropping or spilling?" Dallas had once asked Mr. Trepid.

"Thinking Corner. Two hours," was Mr. Trepid's reply.

As he sat in the dark corner of the basement, Dallas imagined a broad field rimmed with trees, and in that imaginary field he ran and shouted and threw sticks and mud, and when he was tired, he lay down in the green grass and felt himself getting smaller and smaller until he was a little baby lying in the grass, and someone with a sweet face leaned down and wrapped him in a white blanket.

When Florida was caught breaking the rules, she was more likely to argue and, as a result, to earn extra punishments. She could not sit still, could not walk when her feet wanted to run, and so on a fairly regular basis, she'd be running down the hall and Mrs. Trepid's long skinny arm would dart out from a doorway, snare Florida, and lead her to the nearest copy of The Rules.

"What does that say?" Mrs. Trepid demanded.

Florida squinted at the sign. "No stupid running."

"It does not say that," Mrs. Trepid said, urging Florida's face closer to the sign. "Read it again."

"No stinking stupid running."

"Down to the basement. Two hours in the Thinking Corner."

"That's stupid."

"Followed by two hours of floor scrubbing."

1. Based on information from both passages, which statement best expresses how Rodzina, Dallas, and Florida feel about the adults who watch over them?
   Ⓐ They think the adults have a huge responsibility.
   Ⓑ They think the adults are heartless and mean.
   Ⓒ They think the adults have an easy life.
   Ⓓ They think the adults are busy and tired.

2. Which excerpt from Passage 1 supports the answer to question 1?
   Ⓐ "One woman, burdened with children, blankets, a tin kettle, and a three-legged stove, finally put that stove right down on the platform, sat herself atop it, and began to cry."
   Ⓑ "He tipped his hat again."
   Ⓒ "I finally gathered that she was from the Orphan Asylum and was calling us all together."
   Ⓓ "She was pale and thin, her mouth ill-humored, and her gray eyes as cold and sharp as the wire rims of her spectacles."

3. Which excerpt from Passage 2 supports the answer to question 1?
   Ⓐ "'If we didn't have rules,' Mr. Trepid liked to say, 'everything would be chaos.'"
   Ⓑ "The managers of the Home, Mr. and Mrs. Trepid, were middle-aged, cranky and tired, and growing stiff and cold as winter-bound trees."
   Ⓒ "'If we didn't have rules,' his wife would say, 'these children would eat us alive.'"
   Ⓓ "Since Dallas and Florida had lived in the Boxton Creek Home longer than any of the other children there, they knew all the rules."

4. Why does the narrator share Dallas and Florida's differing reactions to being told to go to the Thinking Corner? Use evidence from the passage to support your response.

_____

_____

_____

_____

5. Read these excerpts from both passages:

"On a cold Monday morning in March, when a weak, pale sun struggled to shine and ice glistened in the cracks in the wooden street, a company of some twenty-two orphan children with stiff new clothes and little cardboard suitcases boarded a special railway car at the station near the Chicago River."

"Boxton was a tired town, a neglected place that looked as if it was in danger of collapsing in on itself. A tangle of old homes and shacks clustered around small stores and buildings that had seen better days. One of these buildings was the Boxton Creek Home for Children, a ramshackle house that tilted toward the train tracks and hills beyond."

These excerpts are used mainly to
Ⓐ show the weather in both passages
Ⓑ set the tone for the main characters' experiences as orphans
Ⓒ describe the time period of each passage
Ⓓ illustrate the differences between Chicago and the Boxton Creek Home

6. How does Dallas' daydream in the Thinking Corner compare to his reality at the Boxton Creek Home? Provide evidence from the story to support your response.

_____

_____

_____

_____

(Answers are on page 61.)

SUMMARIZE AND EXPLAIN RELATIONSHIPS

RI.5.2 Determine two or more main ideas of a text and explain how they are supported by key details; summarize the text.

RI.5.3 Explain the relationships or interactions between two or more individuals, events, ideas, or concepts in a historical, scientific, or technical text based on specific information in the text.

Directions: Read the following passage from *Whales* by Judith Hodge. Then answer the following questions about the passage.

Introduction

Whales are monarchs among the animals of the oceans. They are some of the most enormous—and most intelligent—animals on earth. The blue whale, for example, is the largest animal that has ever lived. Full grown, it can be nearly one hundred feet long and weigh one hundred and fifty tons.

The first surprising fact about whales is that they are not fishes. They certainly look like fishes, and they do live in the sea. But they are mammals, like humans.

What distinguishes whales from fishes? There are a number of clues. Fishes extract oxygen from the water through gills. Whales come to the surface to take in air, and they breathe using lungs.

Whales are warm-blooded. This means that their body temperature remains relatively constant. Fishes, on the other hand, are cold-blooded. Their body temperature changes according to the temperature of their environment.

Humpback Whales

Humpback whales have only a small hump at the back of the head. They are distinguished more readily by their very long flippers, which can almost be as long as a third of their bodies. These are used for steering and for "flippering," making loud splashing noises with their flippers on the water, probably to communicate with other humpbacks.

Humpbacks are also famous for another form of communication, their singing. Male humpbacks sing for hours to attract females. Scientists can tell where a whale comes from by its song, as distinctive tunes are sung by different humpback populations.

Blue Whales

There is no mistaking a blue whale. It's not only blue, it's BIG and blue. In fact, blue whales are the largest living creatures on the planet. At one hundred feet long and weighing over two hundred tons, they make the largest living land animal, the elephant, look puny! At birth, a baby blue whale is already as big as a fully-grown elephant.

Newborn blue whales feed on their mother's milk until they are six or seven months old—over twenty-five gallons every day! The milk has a very high fat content, so the baby grows quickly. By the time it is weaned it is already fifty feet long.

Unfortunately, their huge size made blue whales easy targets for hunting. They were protected in the mid-1960s, by which point it is estimated that over a third of a million blue whales had been killed. Whale populations in some oceans may never recover from such intense whaling.

History of Whaling

Whales have been hunted since prehistoric times: a four thousand-year old Norwegian rock drawing shows whaling scenes. Many products were made from whales, such as brushes and corsets from baleen and oil for lamps and candles. The greatest disaster for whale numbers came in the early 1900s with the factory ships. These enormous boats, equipped with spotter plans and sonar tracking equipment, processed dead whales at sea. Between 1900 and 1940 more whales were slaughtered than in the previous four hundred years! The International Whaling Commission (IWC) was set up in 1946 to regulate the whaling industry, but continued to set quotas that were too high until the 1970s. By 1986 there was a worldwide ban on whaling—there were too few whales left for it to be sustainable.

The Future for Whales

Public opinion played an important part in the ban on commercial whaling. Campaigns by conservation groups have done much to turn the tide against whaling in many countries.

However, most of the whale species that were commercially hunted, such as the blue, bowhead, and right whales, are still on the endangered list. The numbers of some species are so low that they may never recover. Blue whales, for example, have been protected for several decades. Some other species, such as beaked whales, have always been very rare.

Hope for the whale's future could lie in the rise of interest in whale-watching. There are now a number of countries worldwide where tourists can catch a glimpse of whales in their natural habitat.

1. Which of these is one of the main ideas of the passage?
   Ⓐ People like to hunt whales for various reasons.
   Ⓑ Whales are fascinating animals and should be protected.
   Ⓒ Humpback whales have a lot in common with blue whales.
   Ⓓ Millions of years ago, whales used to live on land like other mammals.

2. According to the passage, what two factors helped ban commercial whaling?

   _____   _____

3. Read this sentence from the passage:

   "Scientists can tell where a whale comes from by its song, as **distinctive** tunes are sung by different humpback populations."

   The word **distinctive** means
   - Ⓐ similar
   - Ⓑ loud
   - Ⓒ unclear
   - Ⓓ special

4. Read this sentence from the passage:

   "By 1986 there was a worldwide ban on whaling—there were too few whales left for it to be **sustainable**."

   The word **sustainable** means
   - Ⓐ able to get weaker
   - Ⓑ able to be stopped
   - Ⓒ able to be kept at a certain level
   - Ⓓ able to get smaller

5. According to the passage, what served as the greatest threat to whale numbers?
   - Ⓐ scientific research
   - Ⓑ high quotas
   - Ⓒ factory ships
   - Ⓓ lack of krill

6. Why does the author talk about fish in the introduction? Provide evidence from the passage to support your response.

   _____

   _____

   _____

7. How does the flippering of a humpback whale compare to the singing of a humpback whale? Provide evidence from the passage to support your response.

_____

_____

_____

8. Read this sentence from the passage:

   "Fishes **extract** oxygen from the water through gills."

   What does the word **extract** mean in this sentence?

   _____

9. Read this excerpt from the passage:

   "At one hundred feet long and weighing over two hundred tons, they make the largest living land animal, the elephant, look puny! At birth, a baby blue whale is already as big as a fully-grown elephant."

   The author uses a comparison between blue whales and elephants to
   Ⓐ illustrate the similarities between the two
   Ⓑ emphasize the blue whale's size
   Ⓒ explain that elephants can be puny
   Ⓓ point out how much a baby blue whale eats

10. Why did the author most likely include background information on the history of whaling and on the whales' future? Provide evidence from the passage to support your response.

    _____

    _____

    _____

(Answers are on page 62.)

ANALYZE PAIRED TEXTS AND SUPPORT WITH EVIDENCE

RI.5.6 Analyze multiple accounts of the same event or topic, noting important similarities and differences in the point of view they represent.

RI.5.8 Explain how an author uses reasons and evidence to support particular points in a text, identifying which reasons and evidence support which point(s).

Directions: Read the following passages from *What's the Point of Being Green?* by Jacqui Bailey and "*There's No Meat in Chocolate Cake*" by Maryrose Wood. Then answer the following questions about the passages.

Passage 1

A Growing Problem

[There is a problem with] the way we grow our food. Although improvements in farming mean that we can now grow and harvest more food than ever before, there is a downside.

Using fertilizers to help crops grow, and sprays to kill pests and diseases guarantees bigger and better crops but pollutes our air, water, and soil. And when soil is made to grow crops too quickly, it can become exhausted and lacking in nutrients, which makes it unable to grow anything at all. When crops fail, people and animals starve and the soil turns to dust, leaving it open to erosion by wind and rain.

Also, clearing land to grow crops for business or biofuels or to use as grazing land for cattle ranches is a major cause of deforestation and loss of habitats such as grasslands. This not only affects wildlife but can mean that local people are no longer able to use the land as a source of food for themselves.

Can't Someone Invent Something?

You might think that because scientific improvements helped get us into this mess, scientists should help get us out of it. The problem is that, as we have learned, new inventions can bring unexpected changes in the future.

One thing that scientists are doing is looking for ways to make food plants stronger and more able to survive in worsening climate conditions. This means developing plants that can grow in dry conditions, for example, or in saltier soil along coastlines—or that need less fertilizer to make them grow, or fewer pesticides. Some scientists are even trying to produce meat without rearing animals.

New Foods

Changing food plants and creating new types of food in this way is called genetic modification, or GM for short. Some people are afraid of GM foods and worry that these changes could damage our health or the environment in the future. Others say that farmers have been changing and improving our food crops for years and it makes no difference if it is done in a laboratory or in a field.

For better or worse, however, it is clear that GM foods can make a difference to the quality and amount of food we can grow.

Cupboard Love

But science cannot give us all the answers. To make the right decisions about what we eat, we need to know how our food is produced and where it comes from. And we should remember that food and water are precious resources.

And we can try to...

Think more carefully about the food we buy—and waste less of it. It would also help if we made even small changes to our diet. Eat more vegetables and give up meat even once or twice a week, for example, and choose sustainable fish.

Buy local, seasonal food whenever we can. When we do buy food from other countries, we could try to support small farmers working in poor countries. At the moment, the best way to do that is to buy products that carry the Fair Trade Certified label on them. Fair Trade is about making sure that small-scale farmers and workers in developing countries receive a fair price for their products, as well as a Fair Trade premium, which farmers and workers can invest in projects to improve the lives of their families and communities.

Passage 2

I am every grandmother's worst nightmare—the Thanksgiving dinner guest who does not eat turkey.

"But it's Thanksgiving!" I used to hear, before my family finally got used to my eating habits. "You have to eat some turkey!"

No, I did not. And I do not. I've been a vegetarian for nearly twenty-five years now, and during that entire time I've subsisted happily on good healthy vegetarian foods. Like chocolate cake and pizza.

Now, I don't think everyone should be a vegetarian. But eating less meat is not only good for your health, it's good for the environment, too.

Why? Think about the cow that turned into the hamburger you ate yesterday. That cow had been eating like—well, like a cow, since the day it was born. Chances are it weighed more than a thousand pounds by the time it was prematurely sent to cow heaven, so you can imagine how many calories it had consumed in its life. Gazillions, I think is the precise answer.

Those calories probably came from commercially grown feed made of corn and soy and lots of additives. The corn and soybeans were most likely grown with the use of tons of chemical fertilizers, much of which ran off into nearby lakes and rivers. Yuck!

The additives might include things like hormones to make the cows fatten up faster and antibiotics to prevent the cows from getting sick when eating the feed. Why does the feed make them sick? you ask. Because cows are designed to graze on grass, not eat weird chemical-laced feed. If you think about that for a while your head will hurt, I promise.

Feeding a cow gazillions of calories just so a roomful of humans can enjoy a steak dinner is an incredibly wasteful way to make food. Someone once figured that twenty vegetarians could live off the land required to feed one meat eater. Reducing our meat consumption even a small amount would free up millions of tons of grain, enough to feed whole nations full of hungry people.

And OMG! Don't forget the trees! Millions of acres of forests have been cut down to make room for cattle grazing. Those forests make oxygen, which is kind of important. The cows make methane-filled burps and farts, which contribute to global warming. It's a no-brainer, people!

I'm picking on cows here, but the same is true for all kinds of animals that are commercially raised for human consumption. And guess what? Everything the cow (or pig, or chicken) ate ends up in that nice hormone-and-antibiotic-flavored meat meal on your plate, and soon in you. Pizza, anyone?

Eating less meat is easy to do, and veggies and grains and legumes are delicious! When you or your parents do shop for meat (or eggs, or even milk), buy products that are not from the big corporate meat-factory world that stuffs animals with feed full of toxic chemicals. Look for labels like "organic," "free-range," "grass-fed," and "no hormones or antibiotics used." It will likely cost a bit more, but you're going to eat less of it, so it will all balance out.

And try to be a vegetarian for a couple of meals (or maybe even a couple of days) a week. The chocolate cake is waiting.

1. What is one of the main ideas in both passages?
   Ⓐ The earth is in danger, and there is not much that can be done to reverse the damage.
   Ⓑ Since cows are releasing too much methane in the air, more trees should be planted to produce the oxygen we need.
   Ⓒ Although there are some environmental concerns with the way humans farm plants and animals, people can take steps to address these problems.
   Ⓓ Scientists are working hard to find solutions to environmental threats.

2. Which statement best summarizes the authors' points of view in both passages?
   Ⓐ The author of Passage 1 implies that the way we grow our food does not impact wildlife, while the author of Passage 2 highlights the effects it has on animals.
   Ⓑ The author of Passage 2 suggests that environmental threats only affect people in the United States, while the author of Passage 1 explains how environmental threats impact farmers in poor countries.
   Ⓒ Both authors feel that aggressive farming has improved our lifestyles over the years.
   Ⓓ Both authors believe that there is a problem with the way we grow our food.

3. Which section from Passage 1 is most similar to the last two paragraphs of Passage 2? Provide evidence from the passages to support your response.

   _____

   _____

   _____

4. How are Passage 1 and Passage 2 different?
   Ⓐ Passage 1 encourages people to help improve the environmental problem.
   Ⓑ Passage 1 describes how deforestation impacts the environmental problem.
   Ⓒ Passage 2 includes the author's own views on the environmental problem.
   Ⓓ Passage 2 provides details on how scientists are trying to solve the environmental problem.

5. Read this excerpt from Passage 2:

> "Feeding a cow gazillions of calories just so a roomful of humans can enjoy a steak dinner is an incredibly wasteful way to make food. Someone once figured that twenty vegetarians could live off the land required to feed one meat eater."

What does the author hope to achieve by using number words in this excerpt?

_____

_____

_____

6. Which sentence(s) from Passage 1 best support(s) the author's claim that producing quick-growing crops could be harmful?

_____

_____

_____

7. Read this excerpt from Passage 1:

> "Also, clearing land to grow crops for business or biofuels or to use as grazing land for cattle ranches is a major cause of deforestation and loss of habitats such as grasslands."

Write the line(s) from Passage 2 that best support(s) this excerpt.

_____

_____

_____

8. Read this excerpt from Passage 1:

> "Changing food plants and creating new types of food in this way is called genetic modification, or GM for short. Some people are afraid of GM foods and worry that these changes could damage our health or the environment in the future. Others say that farmers have been changing and improving our food crops for years and it makes no difference if it is done in a laboratory or in a field."

This excerpt is used mainly to
Ⓐ compare two points of view on GM
Ⓑ illustrate the effectiveness of GM
Ⓒ describe those who are opposed to GM
Ⓓ present the reasons why more people eat genetically modified foods

9. Why does the author of Passage 2 most likely end with the sentence, "The chocolate cake is waiting"?

_____

_____

_____

(Answers are on page 63.)

29

NARRATIVES

W.5.3 Write narratives to develop real or imagined experiences or events using effective technique, descriptive details, and clear event sequences.
W.5.4 Produce clear and coherent writing in which the development and organization are appropriate to task, purpose, and audience.

Directions: Read the writing situation and task below. Then write your response on the lines provided.

WRITING SITUATION

Jacob is outside one day, playing hide-and-seek with his brother. As Jacob searches for the perfect hiding place, he spies an old metal box hidden in the trunk of a tree. Jacob lifts the box, opens the lid, and looks inside. He quickly realizes that this metal box is special.

WRITING TASK

Write a story for your teacher about what Jacob finds in the old metal box and the events that follow.

_____

_____

_____

_____

_____

_____

_____

_____

_____

_____

_____

_____

_____

_____

_____

_____

_____

_____

_____

_____

_____

_____

_____

_____

_____

_____

_____

_____

_____

_____

_____

_____

_____

_____

_____

_____

_____

(Sample answer is on page 63.)

OPINION PIECES

W.5.1 Write opinion pieces on topics or texts, supporting a point of view with reasons and information.

W.5.4 Produce clear and coherent writing in which the development and organization are appropriate to task, purpose, and audience.

Directions: Read the writing situation and task below. Then write your response on the lines provided.

WRITING SITUATION

Some experts say that kids spend too much time in front of a computer, tablet, and/or smartphone screen. They think that kids should be limited to a certain amount of "screen" time each day. Some kids agree with this idea while others disagree.

Your teacher has asked you to write an essay expressing your opinion about this topic.

WRITING TASK

Write an essay for your teacher expressing your opinion about limiting "screen" time for kids. Be sure to use reasons, facts, and examples to support your position.

_____

_____

_____

_____

_____

_____

_____

_____

_____

_____

_____

_____

(Sample answer is on page 64.)

INFORMATIVE/EXPLANATORY TEXTS

W.5.2 Write informative/explanatory texts to examine a topic and convey ideas and information clearly.

W.5.4 Produce clear and coherent writing in which the development and organization are appropriate to task, purpose, and audience.

Directions: Read the writing situation and task below. Then write your response on the lines provided.

WRITING SITUATION

Writer Mark Twain once said, "Kindness is a language that the deaf can hear and the blind can see." Think about what Mark Twain is saying about how people can use kindness to affect someone's life.

WRITING TASK

Write an essay where you explain how people can use kindness to affect someone's life. Use your knowledge of books, current events, famous people, or your own experiences or observations to develop your essay. Be sure to include details, reasons, and examples to support your explanation.

(Sample answer is on page 65.)

ENGLISH LANGUAGE ARTS PRACTICE TEST

My Name: _____

Today's Date: _____

Directions: Circle the appropriate conjunction or correlative conjunction to be used in each sentence.

1. Kenyatta found a kitten in the park, (so/but) he brought it home to feed it.

2. Lin found (not only/either) the game he had lost (nor/but also) the new controller.

Directions: Circle the preposition(s) or interjection in each sentence.

3. Marilyn walked toward the teacher with her homework.

4. Hey, could you help me with this heavy box?

5. Anne jumped over the bushes to catch her rabbit.

Directions: Circle the appropriate perfect verb tense to be used in each sentence.

6. Bruno (has brushed/had brushed/will have brushed) his teeth before he climbed into bed.

7. The washing machine (has washed/had washed/will have washed) most of the clothes already.

Directions: Circle the verb. Then write if the verb in each sentence is in the present, past, or future tense.

8. Ebony kicked the football more than fifty yards during last week's semifinal game.

    _____

9. My cousin will buy me a game for my birthday next week.

    _____

Directions: Rewrite the following sentences, replacing the underlined word with the verb in the appropriate tense.

10. Last week, Marie weeded the garden and <u>plants</u> new vegetables.

_____

_____

11. Ramon eats his favorite cereal and <u>will watch</u> cartoons on television.

_____

_____

Directions: Rewrite the following sentences using appropriate punctuation and capitalization.

12. there are twenty-five students in mrs miller's class at busy bee academy

_____

_____

13. why aren't you going to the museum of natural history next tuesday

_____

_____

Directions: Finish each sentence by filling in the correctly spelled word.

14. A scientist needs all of the _____ materials to conduct an experiment properly.
    Ⓐ necessary   Ⓑ nessesery   Ⓒ necuhsarry

15. Tsunamis, tornadoes, and hurricanes are examples of _____ weather patterns.
    Ⓐ seveere   Ⓑ suhveere   Ⓒ severe

Directions: Read each sentence. Add commas where necessary to create a grammatically correct sentence.

16. See I told you that you would do well on your test!

17. Matt's favorite animals are tigers dolphins and sharks.

18. Jenna what time do you want to go to the game?

19. Maria Pat and Kathy went to the museum to see the exhibit.

45

Directions: Read the sentence and select the best definition for the word in bold. Underline the context clues (words or phrases) that helped you determine the word's meaning.

20. It was cloudy and rainy all day, making it a very **dismal** Sunday.
    Dismal most likely means
    Ⓐ lively
    Ⓑ gloomy
    Ⓒ cold
    Ⓓ perky

21. The summer lifeguards were **sweltering** on the beach during the long heat wave.

    Sweltering most likely means _____

Directions: Use your knowledge of common Greek and Latin affixes and roots to help determine the meaning of the words in bold.

22. The swim instructor taught the children how to **submerge** themselves in the pool so only the tops of their heads could be seen.

    What is the meaning of the affix, *sub*-?
    Ⓐ above   Ⓑ under   Ⓒ across

23. *Submerge* most likely means
    Ⓐ under water
    Ⓑ above water
    Ⓒ through water
    Ⓓ outside of water

24. We had to **vacate** the school during the fire drill.

    What is the meaning of the root word, **vac**-?
    Ⓐ fill   Ⓑ walk   Ⓒ empty

25. *Vacate* most likely means
    Ⓐ to walk around in
    Ⓑ to make a place full
    Ⓒ to remain
    Ⓓ to leave a place

Directions: Read each sentence and determine if a simile or metaphor is being used. Then explain the meaning of the simile or metaphor.

26. During the holiday season, the local mall is crazy like a zoo.
    Ⓐ simile   Ⓑ metaphor

    Explain the meaning of the expression.

    _____

    _____

27. My brother is a ball of energy when he eats a lot of sugar.
    Ⓐ simile   Ⓑ metaphor

    Explain the meaning of the expression.

    _____

    _____

Directions: Explain the meaning of the idiom, adage, or proverb used in each sentence.

28. Elizabeth **bent over backward** to help me sell the last batch of cookies.

    Explain the meaning of the expression.

    _____

    _____

29. The broken glass sent up a **red flag** that something was wrong.

    Explain the meaning of the expression.

    _____

    _____

Directions: Read each sentence to find the meaning of the underlined word. Use the words in italics as a clue.

30. We decided to look through the microscope to find <u>minute</u> details that were otherwise *too hard to see*.

    <u>Minute</u> most likely means
    (A) bright
    (B) large
    (C) wavy
    (D) tiny

31. Colin found a piece of <u>ancient</u> furniture in the basement that must be from *100 years ago*.

    <u>Ancient</u> most likely means
    (A) modern
    (B) old
    (C) dusty
    (D) dark

Directions: Read the following passage from *The Penderwicks* by Jeanne Birdsall. Then answer the following questions about the passage.

Skye reached through the fence and scratched Hound's nose. "Daddy, I'm going exploring. Is that okay?"

"As long as you're back in an hour for dinner. And Skye, *quidquid agas prudenter agas et respice finem*."

Mr. Penderwick didn't use Latin just for plants, but in his everyday speech, too. He said that it kept his brain properly exercised. Much of the time his daughters had no idea what he was talking about, but Skye was used to hearing this phrase, which Mr. Penderwick translated loosely as "look before you leap and please don't do anything crazy."

"Don't worry, Daddy," she said, and meant it. Sneaking into that Mrs. Tifton's gardens, which is what Skye planned to do, wasn't crazy. On the other hand, it wasn't the most correct thing—according to Harry the Tomato Man—but maybe he'd been wrong. Maybe Mrs. Tifton loved having strangers wandering around her gardens. After all, anything's possible, thought Skye, and off she went, waving good-bye to her father and Hound.

The land surrounding the cottage was large enough for three or four soccer fields. Not that anyone could play a normal game of soccer there, thought Skye—too many trees. They grew thickest behind the cottage, and the spaces between were filled with nasty, thorny underbrush. The land in front was much more inviting. Here the trees were farther apart, and pretty grasses and wildflowers grew among them.

On one side of the property, a high stone wall separated the cottage from its neighbors. Along the front and the other side ran a boundary hedge. Skye knew that

Mrs. Tifton's gardens were beyond that hedge. She had two options for getting there. She could walk back up the driveway and through the break in the hedge. Boring, and likely to lead to being caught—it's hard to hide on a driveway. Or she could crawl through the hedge and emerge in some sheltered garden nook where neither Mrs. Tifton nor anyone else would be likely to see her.

Definitely option two, Skye decided, veering away from the driveway and toward the hedge. But she found the hedge to be thicker and more prickly than she had anticipated, and after several attempts to crawl through, she had accomplished nothing except snagging her hat twice and scratching her arms until it looked like she had fought a tiger.

Then, when she was just about to give up and go around by the driveway, she discovered a way in. It was a tunnel, carefully hidden behind a clump of tall wildflowers and just the right size for going through on all fours. Now, if Rosalind had been the first to discover that tunnel, she would have noticed that it was too neatly trimmed and pricker-free to be there by mistake, and she would have figured that someone used it often and that the someone probably wasn't Mrs. Tifton. If Jane had been the first, she, too, would have realized that natural forces hadn't formed that tunnel. Her explanation for it would have been nonsense—an escape route for convicts on the run or talking badgers—but at least she would have thought about it. But this was Skye. She only thought, I need a way through the hedge, and here it is. And then she plunged.

32. It can be inferred that the reason why Skye would have to sneak into Mrs. Tifton's gardens is because
   Ⓐ Skye is following her dad's rules
   Ⓑ Mrs. Tifton is not very friendly
   Ⓒ Harry the Tomato Man is looking out for her
   Ⓓ the garden is a shortcut to the cottage

33. Which line(s) from the story best support(s) the answer to question 32?

   _____

   _____

   _____

34. Read this sentence from the story:

   "Definitely option two, Skye decided, **veering** away from the driveway and toward the hedge."

   What is the meaning of the word **veering** as it is used in this sentence?

   _____

35. Read this excerpt from the story:

"Sneaking into that Mrs. Tifton's gardens, which is what Skye planned to do, wasn't crazy. On the other hand, it wasn't the most correct thing—according to Harry the Tomato Man—but maybe he'd been wrong. Maybe Mrs. Tifton loved having strangers wandering around her gardens. After all, anything's possible, thought Skye, and off she went, waving good-bye to her father and Hound."

What could be inferred about Skye based on her words, "After all, anything's possible"?

_____

_____

_____

36. Read this excerpt from the story:

"On one side of the property, a **high stone wall** separated the cottage from its neighbors. Along the front and the other side ran a **boundary hedge**. Skye knew that Mrs. Tifton's gardens were beyond that hedge."

How do the **high stone wall** and **boundary hedge** contribute to the reader's understanding of Mrs. Tifton?

_____

_____

_____

37. Read this excerpt from the story:

"But she found the hedge to be thicker and more prickly than she had **anticipated**, and after several attempts to crawl through, she had accomplished nothing except snagging her hat twice and scratching her arms until it looked like she had fought a tiger."

What is the meaning of the word **anticipated** as it is used in this sentence?

_____

38. The narrator of the story is able to see into Skye's mind, sharing Skye's thoughts with the reader. How does this point of view influence the story?
    (A) The reader remains unaware of the true dangers involved in sneaking around Mrs. Tifton's gardens.
    (B) The reader is able to get a sense of Skye's relationship with her sisters.
    (C) The reader is unable to learn about Skye's true thoughts about sneaking around Mrs. Tifton's gardens.
    (D) The reader understands why Mr. Penderwick does not want his daughters to go exploring.

39. What is the narrative structure of this story?
    (A) circular
    (B) framed
    (C) fractured
    (D) chronological

40. Read this excerpt from the story:

    "But this was Skye. She only thought, I need a way through the hedge, and here it is. And then she **plunged**."

    What is the meaning of the word **plunged** as it is used in this sentence?
    (A) moved carefully
    (B) hesitated for a moment
    (C) entered suddenly
    (D) climbed up

41. The descriptions of Rosalind and Jane in the last paragraph are used to point out
    (A) Skye's impulsivity
    (B) that Skye is younger than her sisters
    (C) how Rosalind and Jane feel about the tunnel
    (D) the relationship between the sisters

Directions: Read the following passage from *A Day in the Life of Your Body* by Beverly McMillan. Then answer the following questions about the passage.

Rise and Shine!

When you wake up, you become aware of the world around you, thanks to signals from your body's neurons, or nerve cells. Nerve cells in the brain and in the spinal cord, running down your spine, form the central nervous system. Long cable-like extensions of nerve cells are bundled into nerves. They run through the rest of your body and form the peripheral nervous system. Nerves bring information from your eyes and other sensory organs to the brain. They also carry orders from the brain and spinal cord to your muscles and internal organs. Your endocrine system makes chemicals called hormones that work with the brain to control many functions.

Waking the Brain

Brain scans provide an amazing window into how the brain works. Some parts of the brain are most active when you are asleep while others shift into higher gear as you wake up. A ringing alarm clock or sun streaming in a window is a signal for the brain to begin managing the physical and mental activity that will get you through your day.

Accidents Do Happen

Ouch! A cut hurts! It may also be a danger to your body. Even small cuts and scratches can let in microbes that may cause an infection. Luckily, the body has strong defenses that are always at hand to help keep you healthy. Unbroken skin stops many intruders in their tracks. Chemicals in your saliva and tears also fight microbes. Most important, you have an immune system that can protect you from many diseases. It works together with the lymphatic system. Your white blood cells are some of the body's main defenders. Some kinds make chemicals called antibodies that help to fight invaders. Others are like scouts that find and kill cells infected by bacteria or a virus.

Sneaky Virus

A virus is like a pirate that sneaks into body cells and attacks them. When you have a cold or the flu, a virus is often the culprit. Some kinds of white blood cells can fight viruses by destroying infected cells. The virus, hiding inside, is destroyed, too.

All in the Family

How did you get the shape of your nose or the color of your eyes? You inherited genes from your parents. Genes give the "orders" for building and running your body from head to toe. You have about 19,500 different genes, and all of them are made from a chemical called DNA. DNA is amazing—it can give instructions for making all the different parts of your body and for all the jobs they must do. Your genes aren't all lumped together, however. They are divided into groups, a bit like separate strings of braids. Each group of genes is called a chromosome. There are 23 kinds of chromosomes. Like shoes, you have pairs of them—one from your mother and one from your father.

Staying Fit and Healthy

How can you make sure that every day is a good one for your body? Eating well is a great start. Nutritious foods give you vitamins, minerals, and other raw materials your cells need to work properly. The body also uses water in many ways. Drinking plenty of healthy liquids ensures that your cells and tissues will have the water they need. Being active in the playground and at home will help keep your muscles, bones, and other parts strong and healthy. A good night's sleep will keep your brain sharp and let your growing body rest for the good day to come.

Good Sleep

Sleeping is one of the most important things you do. Too little sleep changes the way your brain works. It will be harder to think about schoolwork and you may feel cranky, too. Being tired can also make you clumsy, so you are more likely to stumble or drop things. If you are under the age of 16, you need at least 8–10 hours of sleep most nights.

42. Which of these is one of the main ideas of the passage?
    Ⓐ The human body faces many challenges.
    Ⓑ Scientists do not know much about the human body.
    Ⓒ The human body is an amazing and complex machine.
    Ⓓ The human body is made up of cells.

43. According to the passage, what is the purpose of nerves?

    _____

    _____

    _____

44. According to the passage, what is the purpose of the brain?

    _____

    _____

    _____

45. How do the sections "Staying Fit and Healthy" and "Good Sleep" relate to one another? Provide evidence from the passage to support your response.

    _____

    _____

    _____

46. Why did the author most likely name the fifth section "All in the Family"?

_____

_____

_____

47. Which excerpt best supports the answer to question 46?
  Ⓐ "Genes give the 'orders' for building and running your body from head to toe."
  Ⓑ "You inherited genes from your parents."
  Ⓒ "DNA is amazing—it can give instructions for making all the different parts of your body and for all the jobs they must do."
  Ⓓ "How can you make sure that every day is a good one for your body? Eating well is a great start."

48. Based on the information in the passage, how is a virus like a pirate?
  Ⓐ A virus needs water to move from one cell to another.
  Ⓑ A virus destroys infected cells.
  Ⓒ A virus sneaks into cells and attacks them.
  Ⓓ A virus causes people to become ill.

49. Read this sentence from the passage:

  "Unbroken skin stops many intruders in their tracks."

  Based on this sentence, one may conclude that
  Ⓐ skin helps protect the body from infections and diseases
  Ⓑ tiny cuts cannot get infected
  Ⓒ skin is able to kill viruses on contact
  Ⓓ microbes are not that dangerous to humans

50. Which excerpt best supports the answer to question 49?
  Ⓐ "Chemicals in your saliva and tears also fight microbes."
  Ⓑ "Most important, you have an immune system that can protect you from many diseases."
  Ⓒ "Others are like scouts that find and kill cells infected by bacteria or a virus."
  Ⓓ "Luckily, the body has strong defenses that are always at hand to help keep you healthy."

(Answers are on page 65.)

WRITING: OPINION

Directions: Read the writing situation and task below. Then write your response on the lines provided.

WRITING SITUATION

For years, people have debated over which animal should be named the Most Fascinating Animal in the World. Some people think that dogs are the most interesting, while others pick animals such as anteaters or howler monkeys.

Your teacher has asked you to write an essay expressing your opinion about this topic.

WRITING TASK

Write an essay for your teacher expressing your opinion on which animal should be named the Most Fascinating Animal in the World. Be sure to use reasons, facts, and examples to support your position.

(Sample answer is on page 68.)

_____

_____

_____

_____

_____

_____

_____

_____

_____

_____

_____

_____

_____

_____

ENGLISH LANGUAGE ARTS ANSWERS EXPLAINED

LANGUAGE

Conjunctions, Prepositions, and Interjections, page 2

1. **but** This word shows the opposite. Even though Deepa would love to go on the roller coaster, she is afraid of being up so high. (L.5.1)

2. **or** Marvin has a choice: pasta or leftovers. (L.5.1)

3. **yet** Even though Tricia is good at soccer, her favorite sport is still dance. (L.5.1)

4. **Both/and** Emily and Saahil both went to camp last summer. (L.5.1)

5. **Either/or** There is a choice here. The only way to get an allowance is to do your chores. (L.5.1)

6. **Neither/nor** My uncle cannot go to the movies. Neither can my grandmother. (L.5.1)

7. **around** The word *around* shows the direction that Tanny walked her dog while in the park. (L.5.1)

8. **between** The word *between* shows the position of the marker. (L.5.1)

9. **under** The word *under* shows the direction that Alton went to look for his book. (L.5.1)

10. **Possible answer: Whoa, that was one scary ride!** Write a sentence that shows shock or surprise. (L.5.1)

11. **Possible answer: Oops, I didn't mean to erase the whole thing**. Write a sentence that shows surprise or regret. (L.5.1)

12. **Possible answer: Woohoo, we won a ribbon at the science fair!** Write a sentence that shows happiness. (L.5.1)

Verb Tenses, page 4

1. **will have completed** The phrase *By next winter* shows that this sentence is in the future perfect tense. (L.5.1)

2. **has arrived** The phrase *is now filling up* shows that this sentence is in the present perfect tense. (L.5.1)

3. **had locked** The word *earlier* shows that this sentence is in the past perfect tense. (L.5.1)

4. **spreads, present tense** The word *spreads* shows that this sentence is taking place now, in the present. (L.5.1)

5. **will leave, future tense** The verb form *will leave* shows that the bus has not left yet. Therefore, this sentence is in the future tense. (L.5.1)

6. **walked, past tense** The verb *walked* shows that this sentence has already happened and is in the past tense. (L.5.1)

7. **Every time Aaliyah scored a goal, her team yelled loudly.** Since *scored* is in the past tense, *will yell* also has to be in the past tense. (L.5.1)

8. **The parents will travel by car and the kids will travel by bus.** Since *will travel* is in the future tense, *travels* also has to be in the future tense. (L.5.1)

9. **All of the chimpanzees gather in the jungle and search for ants**. Since *gather* is in the present tense, *searched* also has to be in the present tense. (L.5.1)

10. **Jaden cleaned his room and stacked his books in a neat pile.** Since *cleaned* is in the past tense, *stacks* also has to be in the past tense. (L.5.1)

Capitalization, Punctuation, and Spelling, page 6

1. **(C)** This sentence has the first word and all of the proper nouns capitalized. It also has the correct ending punctuation. (L.5.2)

2. **(A)** This sentence has the first word and all of the proper nouns capitalized. It also has the correct ending punctuation. (L.5.2)

3. **(C)** (L.5.2)

4. **(B)** (L.5.2)

5. **Maya Angelou was a famous African-American poet, author, dancer, singer, and actress.** Commas are used to separate words in a series. (L.5.2)

6. **Yes, I would love to go to the concert with you on Friday!** Commas are used to set off the words *yes* and *no*. (L.5.2)

7. **If you don't study, you will not be ready for the social studies quiz.** Commas are used to separate an introductory element from the rest of the sentence. (L.5.2)

8. **We had pizza, cookies, and cake at Noah's 11th birthday party.** Commas are used to separate words in a series (L.5.2)

9. **Freddy, I never knew you could jump so high!** Commas are used to indicate direct address. (L.5.2)

10. **Come to think of it, I do want to visit the museum in New York City.** Commas are used to separate an introductory element from the rest of the sentence. (L.5.2)

Understanding Vocabulary, page 8

1. **(B) cold** and underline **shiver** Use context clues from the sentence to determine the meaning of *frigid*. Akiko shivers because of the water, indicating that the water is cold. (L.5.4)

2. **(A) competed** and underline **candidates** Use context clues from the sentence to determine the meaning of *vied*. Since both candidates want to become class president, it could be implied that they are both competing for the position. (L.5.4)

3. **Possible answers: positive, good** and underline *sold out in just one day*. If people rushed out to buy the new video game after hearing the reviews (to the point where stores sold out of it), the reviews must have been positive. (L.5.4)

4. **Possible answers: explain, make clear and underline** *did not understand*. If Ezra did not understand the directions, he would have to ask the teacher to explain them again. (L.5.4)

5. **(A)** The affix *trans-* means through. (L.5.4)

6. **(D)** The affix *trans-* means through. Once the window was clean, it was easy to see through. (L.5.4)

7. **(C)** The root word *geo-* means earth. (L.5.4)

8. **(C)** The root word *geo-* means earth. Isabella's mother studies rocks because rocks are part of the earth. (L.5.4)

9. **(B)** The root word *aqu-* means water. (L.5.4)

10. **(A)** Heavy rains would lead to a lot of water being stored in a particular place. (L.5.4)

Figurative Language, page 10

1. **(B) metaphor; Possible explanation: The pieces of the mystery had to be put together to get to the solution, similar to the pieces of a puzzle.** (L.5.5)

2. **(A) simile; Possible explanation: The backpack is so heavy that it would weigh as much as an elephant.** (L.5.5)

3. **(B) metaphor; Possible explanation: Because Leonardo works hard and is respectful to others, he stands out like a shining star.** (L.5.5)

4. **Possible explanation: Something good could be found in a negative situation.** (L.5.5)

5. **Possible explanation: Zora does not always see things the way Abby does. Therefore, she does not always agree with Abby.** (L.5.5)

6. **Possible explanation: Ryan and Angelo remain friends through both good and bad times.** (L.5.5)

7. **(B)** Stefan is the opposite of his sister (as evidenced by the word *but*). If Stefan is *popular*, his sister, who prefers to be alone, would be a private person who keeps to herself. (L.5.5)

8. **(D)** The word *finish* indicates that after the level is completed, I could move to the next round. (L.5.5)

9. **(A)** Knowing that she had to finish her chores first, Esperanza had the opposite of a smile on her face (as evidenced by the phrase *instead of*). (L.5.5)

10. **(C)** The word *smell* gives the student a clue that something fragrant has to do with a scent. If I stop to smell the flowers every day, they must smell pretty good. (L.5.5)

Make Inferences and Determine Word Meaning, page 12

1. **(C)** Solly knows that his piece of bread is pitiful, causing a feeling of sadness or sympathy. The hunk of bread is so small that one may be embarrassed to actually want to protect it. (RL.5.4)

2. **small** The embarrassing (pathetic) thing about the bread is the size of it. Therefore, "small" connects to the correct response from question 3. (RL.5.4)

3. **(A)** When Solly first realizes that Prudence is the voice in the chestnut tree, his heart sinks. This implies that Solly is not happy to come face-to-face with Prudence and dreads talking to her. (RL.5.1)

4. **Your answer should include details about Solly's inner thoughts and actions to suggest that Solly does not want to share his bread with Prudence.** Solly feels protective of his bread, wraps his fingers over it, and hopes to "divert her mind to things other than the crust" by talking about school. He figures that if he distracts Prudence, maybe she will forget about the bread, leaving it all for himself. (RL.5.1)

5. **(B)** Solly and Prudence are not really friends, suggesting that they do not talk often. After Prudence asks if Solly has anything to eat, Solly concludes that that is the only reason why Prudence took time to talk to him. (RL.5.1)

6. **(D)** Even though Prudence is a young girl, she thinks that she is so smart that she does not need to go to school. By saying "I know all I need to know," Prudence shows readers that she is snooty and feels superior to others. (RL.5.4)

7. **Possible answer: The phrase reveals that Prudence's nose is the most dominant feature on her face.** The narrator describes Prudence's nose as being so long and pointed that it stands out among all her other facial features. Hence, her large nose "ruled her face." (RL.5.4)

8. **Your answer should include details about Solly's refusal to tease Prudence and/ or his willingness to talk to Prudence, even though he does not really like her.** For instance, even though the other boys in the village tease Prudence about her nose, Solly never joined in. Readers could conclude that Solly is not a bully and, thus, a good-hearted person. In addition, Solly decides to talk to Prudence instead of running away, even though he was not really friends with Prudence. (RL.5.1)

Compare and Contrast Paired Texts, page 16

1. **(B)** In both passages, the adults are presented as unkind and cold. (RL.5.9)

2. **(D)** The author chooses specific words to paint a negative picture of the adult from the Orphan Asylum. By describing the adult as ill-humored, the author shows readers that the adult is not easily amused. The author also uses distinct adjectives (gray, cold, sharp) to evoke an unfriendly feeling. (RL.5.9)

3. **(B)** Here, the author also chooses specific words to paint a negative picture of Mr. and Mrs. Trepid. Not only are Mr. and Mrs. Trepid cranky and tired, but they were also stiff and

cold. These words bring to mind very unwelcoming characteristics. (RL.5.9)

4. **You should explain that the narrator is showing the differences in their personalities.** In the second paragraph, the narrator specifically describes the differing personalities between Dallas and Florida. By showing readers how the two characters react differently to being told to go to the Thinking Corner, the narrator provides proof of these characteristics. Dallas, the quieter of the two, went to the Thinking Corner as he was told while Florida, whose mouth was "full of words bursting out," talks back to Mrs. Trepid and challenges the rules. (RL.5.3)

5. **(B)** The tone of a story illustrates the attitude of the author and often shapes events by creating a mood. In the first passage, the author uses temperature and weather to paint a dim, dismissal tone, or mood, for the story. The author of the second passage also evokes a depressing tone by describing the town of Boxton as tired and neglected. These excerpts mirror the characters' negative experiences as orphans. (RL.5.9)

6. **Possible answers should compare the lightness of Dallas' daydream with the hard reality of his life at the Boxton Creek Home.** Dallas' daydream shows that Dallas longs for freedom and love. In the daydream, Dallas does things that would get him in trouble in the Boxton Creek Home. He shows his freedom by running, shouting, and throwing sticks and mud without being punished. Once he's grown tired of that, he imagines himself as a baby when someone loves him enough to wrap him in a blanket. The adults at the Boxton Creek Home do not show Dallas this love. (RL.5.3)

Summarize and Explain Relationships, page 20

1. **(B)** A main idea is the most important or central idea of a text. The passage outlines unique characteristics of humpback and blue whales. As the author states, whales are some of the largest animals on earth. The final section of the passage states that "numbers of some species are so low that they may never recover" but there is hope for the whale's future. (RI.5.2)

2. **Public opinion on commercial whaling and campaigns by conservation groups** The first paragraph of the section entitled "The Future for Whales" explicitly states that "Public opinion played an important part in the ban on commercial whaling. Campaigns by conservation groups have done much to turn the tide against whaling in many countries." (RI.5.2)

3. **(D)** The author indicates that different humpback populations sing unique and special songs, allowing scientists to determine which whales live in which areas. (RI.5.4)

4. **(C)** The ban on whaling came about because there were so few whales and they were in danger of being extinct. By stopping people from hunting whales, the International Whaling Commission hoped to protect the whales, allowing them to reproduce and grow in number. (RI.5.4)

5. **(C)** In "History of Whaling" the author states the greatest disaster for whales was the factory ships. (RI.5.2)

6. **Possible answers explain the author writes about fish in the introduction to show that whales are not fish.** The author explains whales are not fishes, and then goes on to discuss the differences between whales and fish. (RI.5.3)

7. **Possible answers should explain that flippering and singing are both forms of communication for the humpback whale.** The author says that humpbacks use flippering to make loud splashes to communicate with other humpbacks. She says, humpbacks are also famous for their singing. (RI.5.3)

8. **Possible answers: withdraw, take out, remove.** Fish breathe by taking oxygen out of the water through their gills. (RI.5.4)

9. **(B)** By comparing a blue whale's size to an elephant, the reader could visualize the enormous size of a blue whale. (RI.5.3)

10. **Possible answers should explain that the author most likely included this information to show readers how the whale population became endangered and why conserva-**

tion efforts should continue. The "History of Whaling" talks about how long whaling has been going on, the products that people make from whales, and how many whales were slaughtered. It also discusses the setup of the International Whaling Commission to protect whales. "The Future for Whales" explains that some whales are still on the endangered list and tells why people should continue to save whales. (RI.5.3)

Analyze Paired Texts and Support with Evidence, page 24

1. **(C)** A main idea is the most important or central idea of a text. Both passages discuss environmental threats that affect the lives of humans and end with ways that people can address these issues. (RI.5.6)

2. **(D)** Both authors center upon problems that exist as a result of the way we grow our food (i.e., fertilizers, deforestation). (RI.5.6)

3. **Cupboard Love** The last two paragraphs of Passage 2 outline ways that humans could eat less meat and chemically-enhanced foods. Similarly, "Cupboard Love" gives suggestions on how we could make better decisions about what we eat. (RI.5.5)

4. **(C)** In Passage 2, the author shares her own views on being a vegetarian for over twenty-five years and how she feels eating less meat could positively impact the environment. In contrast, Passage 1 does not discuss any personal opinions at all. (RI.5.5)

5. **Possible answers should emphasize that the author is using numbers to show that being a vegetarian is more earth-friendly than being a meat eater.** The author of Passage 2 suggests using an overfed cow to feed a roomful of meat eaters is wasteful and, thus, not earth-friendly. Moreover, the author states, "twenty vegetarians could live off the land required to feed one meat eater." This line emphasizes that more people could be fed if they follow a vegetarian diet, making it more earth-friendly. (RI.5.8)

6. **"And when soil is made to grow crops too quickly, it can become exhausted and lacking in nutrients, which makes it unable to grow anything at all."** (RI.5.8)

7. **"Don't forget the trees! Millions of acres of forests have been cut down to make room for cattle grazing."** Passage 1 states that land is cleared to use for grazing land for cattle ranches, which is similar to Passage 2's idea that millions of acres of forests have been cut down to provide more room for cattle to graze, or eat. (RI.5.6)

8. **(A)** The author gives two points of view on GMs. She explains that some people are suspicious of GMs and think GMs may damage our health or environment. In the following sentence, the author says that other people believe that GM foods are similar to a farmer's improving crops and should be allowed. (RI.5.8)

9. **Possible answers should explain that the ending is used to persuade readers to eat less meat.** By ending Passage 2 this way, the author is putting vegetarianism in a positive light. Many children love sweets like chocolate cake. Here she tempts readers to be vegetarian for a couple of meals, which could possibly include chocolate cake (since it is not made from meat). (RI.5.8)

Narratives, page 30

5th grade narrative writing exemplar:

"1...2...3...4...5," Reuven counted slowly.

"I love playing Hide-and-Seek!" Jacob thought to himself as he scrambled around the yard looking for the perfect hiding place. He ran over to the big oak tree and kneeled down.

"Ugh. Reuven will see me here," Jacob whispered. "I should go around to that other tree over in the corner. That one is bigger."

"...6...7...8...9," Reuven continued.

Jacob knew he needed to hurry. Reuven was only counting to twenty. He sprinted to the tree. He walked around it, trying to find a comfortable spot to hide. When he got around to the back of the tree, Jacob accidently kicked something hard.

"Ow!" he yelled. He quickly covered his mouth so Reuven wouldn't hear him. He rubbed his aching toe with one hand and leaned down to pick up the metal box hidden in the tree trunk. The box was shiny and about the size of a box of candy. He turned it over in his hand, wondering what it could be.

"I may love Hide-and-Seek, but I love mysteries even more!" thought Jacob. He lifted the lid and looked inside.

"…19…20! Ready or not, here I come!" Reuven shouted.

"I'm here! Behind the tree in the corner!" said Jacob.

"You're not supposed to tell me!" Reuven whined.

"Just come here! Look at what I found!" Jacob replied anxiously.

In a flash of an eye, Reuven darted over to his brother. Jacob slowly turned to Reuven, his eyes wide.

"What? What is it?" Reuven asked.

"It's a treasure map. Look. Here's a note."

Jacob handed the note to Reuven. He read it out loud. *"Dear lucky one. My name is Tricia. I used to be the local librarian in 1975. I have hidden a very valuable treasure for a lucky person to find. I made a map for you to find the treasure. Good luck."*

Jacob and Reuven looked at each other and smiled. They were always up for an adventure. They both loved exploring and knew the neighborhood really well.

Right away, Jacob and Reuven hopped on a bike and set off to find the treasure. Putting the metal box in his back pocket and holding the fading map in his hands, Jacob called out directions to his brother, who was peddling.

Reuven followed each command and the brothers soon found themselves in front of a tall, brick building.

"That's wacky!" Jacob exclaimed. "The map led us to our school!"

They hopped off the bike and looked at the red X on the map.

"It should be right over…here!" Reuven said, walking three paces to the right.

Jacob and Reuven got down on their knees and started pulling out clumps of grass and dirt with their bare hands. Fifteen minutes passed.

"I think I found something!"

Deep down in the ground, the boys could see a bright green box. They dug even faster and finally lifted up the green box. Excitedly, they opened the box. In the box, wrapped in newspaper, was a whole collection of comic books!

"AWESOME!" Jacob yelled.

"OH YEAH!" Reuven screamed.

Both boys sat down immediately and began to go through the stack. They found first edition comic books with all of their favorite superheroes. They couldn't believe their luck!

After riding back home, telling their parents about the metal box, and reading all of the comics, Jacob and Reuven thought about how much fun they had.

"I know!" said Jacob. "Let's make a new treasure map and bury the comic books in a different spot for someone else to find."

"Yeah!" Reuven agreed.

And that's just what they did.

Opinion Pieces, page 34

5th grade opinion writing exemplar:
Dear Teacher,

It has recently been brought to my attention that some people think that kids spend too much time in front of a screen. They want to limit the amount of "screen" time that kids have. I believe that these people are making a big mistake! They obviously do not understand the benefits of having unlimited screen time.

For one, the Internet is a great source of information and has changed the way people learn in the 21st century. In the past, people may have wondered about something but did not have quick access to the answer. They may try to ask someone else for the information. But what if that person didn't know the answer? They would have to wait for the local library to open, search for a book that may or may not answer their question, and then read the book from front to back, hoping to find the answer. That's a lot of work! Luckily, people nowadays just have to go online, type their question into the search bar, and ta-da! Instant answer.

Another reason why limiting screen time is a bad idea is because kids may miss out on important school notices. Many teachers use websites to post assignments. One time, I had to leave school early to go to the dentist and missed the homework assignment for that day. I was able to go online, check my teacher's website, and get the homework assignment. In addition, teachers often use e-mail to communicate with students after school hours. If screen time was limited, students may miss out on a last-minute notice that the teacher emailed, or be unable to ask their teacher a burning question about an assignment.

Finally, screen time actually brings people together. The people who want to limit screen time often talk about how time in front of a screen isolates people. Well, they're wrong! Many kids play games with their friends online or through apps. For example, my best friend and I play the game Minecraft together. Even if we are in different houses, we can still connect online to build our Minecraft world together. Many games like Minecraft even allow you to chat with your friend! If we were not able to play Minecraft "together," I wouldn't be able to bond with my friend.

Overall, limiting kids' screen time is not a good idea. Spending time in front of a screen can seem like a scary idea for some people but it really is not. Kids use screen time to access important information, stay on top of school assignments, communicate with teachers, and bond with friends through online games or apps. To those people trying to limit kids' screen time I say, "Welcome to the 21st century."

From,
Your Student

Informative/Explanatory Texts, page 38

5th grade informative/explanatory writing exemplar:

Mark Twain once said, "Kindness is a language that the deaf can hear and the blind can see." Kind words or actions can make a huge difference in someone's day. If people showed kindness to others on a daily basis, the world would be a lovely place.

There are lots of children's books that teach people to be kind to others. One book in particular is called *How Full is Your Bucket? For Kids* by Carol McCloud. The book talks about how each person has an invisible bucket. Each time we are kind to someone, we fill that person's bucket! The book encourages children to be kind to others by saying something nice, doing something for someone, and showing love to others.

Sometimes people show kindness after tragic events. For example, Hurricane Sandy destroyed many homes and caused electrical outages across New York and New Jersey. It was one of the worst storms to hit those states in many years. Luckily, people all over the world banded together to help those in need by donating money to the Red Cross, helping to rebuild houses, and delivering food to shelters. Without these acts of kindness, many people would continue to struggle after the storm.

Kindness can also be shown in other ways. Talking to the new boy or girl at school, writing a letter to your grandparents, or doing the dishes for your family without being asked can all make a difference in someone's life. There are times when I offer to make sandwiches for dinner so that my dad can relax after a long day at work. It makes me happy to know that I can make the world a better place simply by being kind.

English Language Arts Practice Test, page 44

1. **so** This word shows a cause/effect relationship. Since Kenyatta found a kitten, he decided to bring it home. (L.5.1)

2. **not only/but also** This choice shows that there was more than one thing found: the game and the controller. (L.5.1)

3. **toward** The word *toward* shows the direction that Marilyn went to hand in her homework. (L.5.1)

4. **hey** The word *hey* is an interjection used to call attention to someone. (L.5.1)

5. **over** The word *over* shows the direction that Anne went to catch her rabbit. (L.5.1)

6. **had brushed** The word *before* shows that this sentence is in the past perfect tense. (L.5.1)

7. **has washed** The word *already* shows that this sentence is in the present perfect tense. (L.5.1)

8. **kicked, past tense** The phrase *last week's* shows that this sentence already happened and is in the past tense. (L.5.1)

9. **will buy, future tense** The phrase *next week* shows that the person's birthday has not happened yet. Therefore, this sentence is in the future tense. (L.5.1)

10. **Last week, Marie weeded the garden and <u>planted</u> new vegetables**. Since *weeded* is in the past tense, *plants* also has to be in the past tense. (L.5.1)

11. **Ramon eats his favorite cereal and <u>watches</u> cartoons on television.** Since *eats* is in the present tense, *will watch* also has to be in the present tense. (L.5.1)

12. **There are twenty-five students in Mrs. Miller's class at Busy Bee Academy.** This sentence has the first word and all of the proper nouns capitalized. It also has the correct ending punctuation. (L.5.2)

13. **Why aren't you going to the Museum of Natural History next Tuesday**? This sentence has the first word and all of the proper nouns capitalized. It also has the correct ending punctuation. (L.5.2)

14. **(A)** (L.5.2)

15. **(C)** (L.5.2)

16. **See, I told you that you would do well on your test!** Commas are used to separate an introductory element from the rest of the sentence. (L.5.2)

17. **Matt's favorite animals are tigers, dolphins, and sharks.** Commas are used to separate words in a series. (L.5.2)

18. **Jenna, what time do you want to go to the game?** Commas are used to indicate direct address. (L.5.2)

19. **Maria, Pat, and Kathy went to the museum to see the exhibit.** Commas are used to separate words in a series (L.5.2)

20. **(B) cloudy and rainy** Students should use context clues from the sentence to determine the meaning of *gloomy*. The clouds and rain make the day dismal, or gloomy. (L.5.4)

21. **Possible answers: sweating, roasting, overheating, boiling hot, burning; during the long heat wave** A heat wave produces very high temperatures. Lifeguards, who spend their days on the beach, would be very hot and sweaty while sitting outside during a heat wave. (L.5.4)

22. **(B)** The affix *sub-* means under or below. (L.5.4)

23. **(A)** The affix *sub-* means under or below. If only the children's heads are showing when they submerge themselves, their bodies must be hidden under water. (L.5.4)

24. **(C)** The root word *vac-* means empty. (L.5.4)

25. **(D)** The root word *vac-* means empty. During a fire drill, the people inside the school have to leave the building for safety. (L.5.4)

26. **(A) Possible answers should explain that the local mall is so busy and crazy during the holiday season, it is like a bunch of wild animals are at a zoo.** (L.5.5)

27. **(B) Possible answers should explain that when the brother is hyped up on sugar, he has a lot of energy balled up inside him.** (L.5.5)

28. **Possible answers should explain that Elizabeth did everything she possibly could to help out.** (L.5.5)

29. **Possible answers should explain that a red flag is a warning sign.** The broken glass was a warning that something bad happened. (L.5.5)

30. **(D)** A microscope helps someone see things up close that are too hard to see, especially things that are tiny. (L.5.5)

31. **(B)** The phrase *100 years ago* indicates that something has been around for a long time and is quite old. (L.5.5)

32. **(B)** Readers could infer that Skye is sneaking into Mrs. Tifton's gardens because Mrs. Tifton is not welcoming to strangers. If Mrs. Tifton were a friendly person, Skye would not have to sneak around to see the garden. (RL.5.1)

33. **"On the other hand, it wasn't the most correct thing—according to Harry the Tomato Man—but maybe he'd been wrong. Maybe Mrs. Tifton loved having strangers**

wandering around her gardens." Harry the Tomato Man warned Skye that sneaking into Mrs. Tifton's gardens wasn't correct. This supports the idea that Mrs. Tifton is not very friendly. (RL.5.1)

34. **Possible answers: turning, moving, swinging, swerving** Skye turns away from the driveway and moves toward the hedge. (RL.5.4)

35. **Possible answers should explain that Skye is an optimist/positive person/person who hopes for the best.** Harry the Tomato Man does not think that Skye should sneak into Mrs. Tifton's gardens. Despite this, Skye says that anything's possible, showing that she is an optimist, a person who hopes for the best. (RL.5.1)

36. **Possible answers should explain that the high stone wall and boundary hedge reinforce the idea that Mrs. Tifton is unfriendly and does not like her neighbors.** Mrs. Tifton surrounds her property with the high stone wall and boundary hedge to keep her neighbors at a distance. (RL.5.5)

37. **Possible answers: expected, predicted, estimated** To anticipate means to expect or predict. Skye thought the hedge would be easy to crawl through, but she soon found out that it was thicker and more prickly than she expected. (RL.5.4)

38. **(A)** The narrator is able to share Skye's thoughts with the reader, leading the reader to see things through Skye's eyes. Since Skye does not think that sneaking into Mrs. Tifton's gardens is crazy, the reader is not aware of the bad things that could happen to her if she gets caught. (RL.5.6)

39. **(D)** A narrative story structure describes how a story develops over the course of a text. A story that is written chronologically follows a specific time sequence and is organized around a series of events. (RL.5.5)

40. **(C)** To plunge means to enter something suddenly, without hesitation or pause. Skye quickly goes through the tunnel. (RL.5.4)

41. **(A)** The passage suggests that Rosalind and Jane would be more observant, or aware, of certain details about the tunnel. Skye does not think like Rosalind or Jane and plunges through the tunnel to get through the hedge. (RL.5.3)

42. **(C)** A main idea is the most important or central idea of a text. Throughout the passage, the author explains different parts of the human body, their functions, and how they work together. (RI.5.2)

43. **Possible answers should state that nerves carry information to and from the brain.** The section "Rise and Shine!" explicitly states nerves bring information to the brain and carry orders from the brain to muscles and internal organs. (RI.5.2)

44. **Possible answers should explain that the brain manages daily physical and mental activities.** The passage explicitly states that the brain manages "the physical and mental activity that will get you through your day." (RI.5.2)

45. **Possible answers should say that both sections discuss important ways to take care of your body.** "Staying Fit and Healthy" suggests why people should eat well and drink healthy liquids. "Good Sleep" explains, the importance of sleep. (RI.5.3)

46. **Possible answers should explain that the author most likely named the section "All in the Family" because the section talks about genes.** Genes stay in the family because a child can only inherit genes from his/her parents. (RI.5.8)

47. **(B)** This sentence clearly supports the idea of genes passing down from parent to child. (RI.5.8)

48. **(C)** The section "Sneaky Virus" explicitly states, "a virus is like a pirate that sneaks into body cells and attacks them." (RI.5.2)

49. **(A)** If skin is able to stop intruders in their tracks, it can be inferred that skin protects the body from microbes that cause infections and diseases. (RI.5.8)

50. **(D)** As explained in the section "Accidents Do Happen," skin tries to defend the body from microbes to keep people healthy and free of infections. (RI.5.1)

Writing: Opinion

5th grade opinion writing exemplar:

Dear Teacher,

Dogs. Anteaters. Howler monkeys. For years, people have debated over which animal is the Most Fascinating Animal in the World. Even though there are thousands of animals out there, I am here to tell you about the most fascinating one of them all: the octopus.

Did you know that the octopus is one of the world's greatest ninjas? (Well, maybe "ninja" is not the most accurate word but it is pretty close.) That's because an octopus can instantly camouflage itself to look like its surroundings. It has special cells and muscles in its skin to quickly match colors and even textures around it. Pretty fascinating, right?

Another fascinating fact about an octopus is that it can squeeze its huge, soft body into the teeniest, tiniest crack ever. This comes in really handy when a shark or predator is chasing it. One minute the octopus is about to be lunch, and the next minute it disappears into a small crack in the coral. Talk about a speedy getaway!

Most people know that an octopus sprays black ink to confuse predators . . . however, most people *don't* know that the ink has a special substance in it that blocks the predator's sense of smell. This makes it even harder for the predator to track the octopus as it swims away. Since many predators use their sense of smell to find food, this trick makes it almost impossible to catch an octopus. In addition, an octopus doesn't use its ink only to get away from dangerous animals. It also uses the ink to confuse animals that it wants to eat, like crabs and clams.

Overall, an octopus is a fascinating animal. It can camouflage into its surroundings, squeeze its body into small places, and use ink to get away from predators. Moreover, the ink has a substance that dulls a predator's sense of smell, making it easier to escape. All of these abilities make the mighty octopus the Most Fascinating Animal in the World.

From,
Your Student

(W.5.1, W.5.4)

Credits

Solomon Snow and the Silver Spoon by Kate Umansky, 2007, Chronicle Books

Rodzina by Karen Cushman, 2003, Clarion Books

Ruby Holler by Sharon Creech, 2002, Harper Collins

Whales (Animals of the Oceans) by Judith Hodge, 1997, Barron's

What's the Point of Being Green? by Jacqui Bailey, 2010, Barron's

"There's No Meat in Chocolate Cake" by Maryrose Wood, from *Recycle This Book: 100 Top Children's Book Authors Tell You How to Go Green,* edited by Dan Gutman, 2009, Yearling

The Penderwicks by Jeanne Birdsall, 2005, Knopf

A Day in the Life of Your Body by Beverly McMillan, 2012, Barron's

MATH

The Common Core mathematics standards are created to be building blocks between grade levels. The concepts learned in grades 3 and 4 are foundational skills necessary for students to master grade 5 concepts. This allows teachers to make sure that achievement gaps are closed and that students have prior knowledge to continue their learning with more challenging concepts.

The Common Core standards in grades 3 and 4 allow students to continue building strong number sense as they learn to order, compare, and compute with large numbers. A student's ability to think about numbers flexibly and to understand the relationships between numbers is imperative to the concepts that are taught throughout all grade levels. In grade 5, students continue to have standards in Operations and Algebraic Thinking, Number and Operations in Base 10, Number and Operations— Fractions, Measurement and Data, and Geometry.

EVALUATE NUMERICAL EXPRESSIONS

> **5.OA.A.1** Use parentheses, brackets, or braces in numerical expressions, and evaluate expressions with these symbols.

1. Using what you know about the properties of operations and order of operations, list the order of steps to evaluate this expression.

$$20 - (3 \times 6) + (15 \div 5) \times 2$$

Step 1: _____   Step 4: _____

Step 2: _____   Step 5: _____

Step 3: _____

2. Follow the steps in question 1 to evaluate the expression. What is the value?

> Remember to complete operations in parentheses first.

3. Which calculation should be done first to simplify this expression?

$$14 + 5 \times (3 + 6) \div 3$$

(A) $14 + 5$

(B) 5×3

(C) $3 + 6$

(D) $6 \div 3$

4. Create a situation in words that would use the following expression to solve:

$$8 \times (6 + 3)$$

5. What is the correct solution when this expression is simplified?

$$2 + 8 \times 6 - [(40 \div 5) - 1]$$

   Ⓐ 3
   Ⓑ 43
   Ⓒ 47
   Ⓓ 53

6. Which is the second step to evaluate this expression?

$$25 \div 5 - 10 \times 3 + 4$$

   Ⓐ $25 \div 5$
   Ⓑ $5 - 10$
   Ⓒ 10×3
   Ⓓ $3 + 4$

7. Place parentheses in this numerical expression so that the value is 12.

$$2 \times 9 \div 3 + 2 \times 3$$

8. Write the following situation using numbers and grouping symbols, then solve.

   Luke has 3 packs of 15 pieces of gum, plus an additional 4 pieces, to share among 7 people.

9. Which expression has a value of 4?
   Ⓐ $3 + 5 \times 2 - 12$
   Ⓑ $13 - 3 \times (4 - 1)$
   Ⓒ $4 \times 8 \div 4 + 2$
   Ⓓ $(7 + 5) \div 2 + 1$

10. Which would be the last operation to compute when evaluating this numerical expression?

$$[24 \div (2 + 10) - 3] \times 2$$

   Ⓐ addition
   Ⓑ subtraction
   Ⓒ multiplication
   Ⓓ division

(Answers are on page 153.)

WRITE AND INTERPRET NUMERICAL EXPRESSIONS

5.OA.A.2 Write simple expressions that record calculations with numbers, and interpret numerical expressions without evaluating them. For example, express the calculation "add 8 and 7, then multiply by 2" as 2 × (8 + 7). Recognize that 3 × (18,932 + 921) is three times as large as 18,932 + 921, without having to calculate the indicated sum or product.

1. Write the numerical expression for

   "The sum of 6 and 4, multiplied by the difference of 15 and 3."

2. How would the following numerical expression be written in words?

   $$7 \times (8 + 3) - 4$$

3. Write the numerical expression for "8 times as large as the difference between 423 and 276."

4. Write the numerical expression (54 + 30) ÷ 12 in words.

5. Which is a correct way of expressing 3 × (534 − 216) + 14?

   Ⓐ 3 times 534, minus 216, plus 14

   Ⓑ the product of 3 and 534, minus the sum of 216 and 14

   Ⓒ 3 times the difference of 534 and 216, plus 14

   Ⓓ 3 times the sum of (534 − 216) and 14

6. Which numerical expression is correct for "18 more than the amount when the sum of 27 and 36 is divided by 9"?

   Ⓐ (27 + 36) ÷ 9 + 18

   Ⓑ 18 + 27 + 36 ÷ 9

   Ⓒ (18 + 27 + 36) ÷ 9

   Ⓓ 27 + 36 ÷ 9 + 18

7. Select all the correctly written expressions for (13 + 35) × (8 − 2).

   ☐ The sum of 13 and 35, multiplied by 8, then subtract 2.

   ☐ Add 13 and 35, subtract 8 and 2, then multiply the sum and difference.

   ☐ The product of the results when 13 is added to 35 and 2 is subtracted from 8.

   ☐ 13 plus 35, times 8, minus 2.

   ☐ Multiply the sum of 13 and 35 by the difference of 8 and 2.

   ☐ Add 13 to 35 multiplied by 8, then subtract 2.

8. How would "6 times as large as the amount when 12 − 5 is added to 15 ÷ 3" be written as a numerical expression? Select all the correct expressions.

   ☐ 6 × 12 − 5 + 15 ÷ 3

   ☐ 6 × (12 − 5) + (15 ÷ 3)

   ☐ 6 × [(12 − 5) + (15 ÷ 3)]

   ☐ [(12 − 5) + (15 ÷ 3)] × 6

9. Write "the quotient of the product of 32 and 15 and the difference of 17 and 9" as a numerical expression.

10. Write 3 × (14 − 5) + 2 × (35 ÷ 5) in words.

(Answers are on page 154.)

ORDERED PAIRS IN THE COORDINATE PLANE

1. Complete the chart by applying the rule to each number.

Rule	0	1	2	3	4	5
Add 2						
Add 4						

2. What is the relationship between the corresponding terms generated by these 2 rules?

_____

_____

_____

_____

3. List the numbers generated in question 1 as ordered pairs. Then graph them on the coordinate plane.

(2, 4), (___ , ___), (___ , ___), (___ , ___), (___ , ___), (___ , ___)

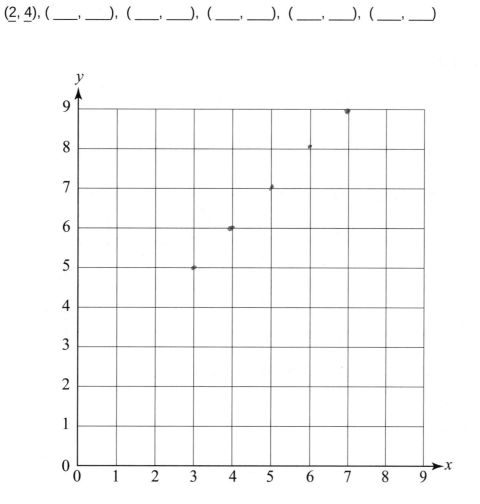

4. Complete the pattern chart.

N	N + 1	N + 5	Ordered Pair
0			
1			
2			
3			
4			
5			

5. Graph the ordered pairs in question 4 below.

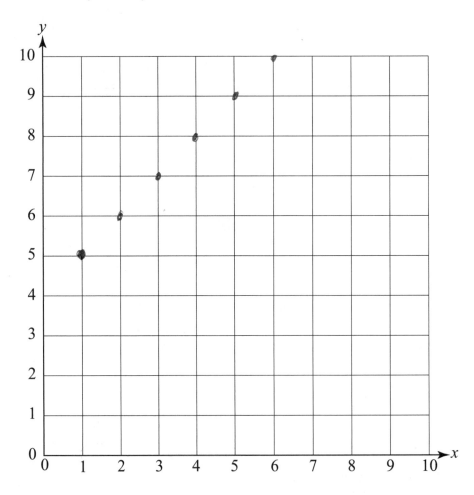

6. What is the relationship between the corresponding terms from the patterns of numbers generated in the chart in question 4?

7. Make a list of numbers using the rules $N \times 4$ and $N \times 2$. (Use the chart in question 4 as a guide.) What is the relationship between the lists of numbers generated by these rules?

8. Create ordered pairs with the lists of the numbers in question 7. Then graph the ordered pairs on the coordinate graph below.

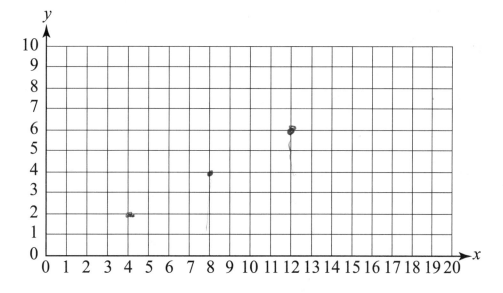

9. Which choice describes the relationship between corresponding terms generated by the rules $N + 2$ and $N + 5$?
   Ⓐ The terms in each ordered pair differ by 2.
   Ⓑ The terms in each ordered pair differ by 3.
   Ⓒ The terms in each ordered pair differ by 7.
   Ⓓ The terms in each ordered pair differ by 10.

10. Which set of ordered pairs has terms in one sequence that are 3 times the corresponding terms in the other sequence?
   Ⓐ (1, 3), (3, 6), (5, 9)
   Ⓑ (1, 4), (2, 5), (3, 6)
   Ⓒ (2, 5), (4, 7), (6, 9)
   Ⓓ (2, 6), (4, 12), (6, 18)

(Answers are on page 155.)

PLACE VALUE

5.NBT.A.1 Recognize that in a multi-digit number, a digit in one place represents 10 times as much as it represents in the place to its right and 1/10 of what it represents in the place to its left.

1. Describe the relationship between 123 and 1,230.

For questions 2–4, what is the relationship between the values of the underlined digits in each pair of numbers?

2. 4<u>3</u> and 4<u>3</u>0

3. 1<u>2</u>3 and 1<u>2</u>30

4. 2.<u>5</u>7 and 2<u>5</u>.7

5. A. Complete the chart. For fraction answers, also show your answers
as decimals.

43 × 1,000	
43 × 100	
43 × 10	
43 × 1	
43 ÷ 10	
43 ÷ 100	
43 ÷ 1,000	

B. Describe the pattern you see in this chart.

(Answers are on page 156.)

MULTIPLY POWERS OF TEN

5.NBT.A.2 Explain patterns in the number of zeros of the product when multiplying a number by powers of 10, and explain patterns in the placement of the decimal point when a decimal is multiplied or divided by a power of 10. Use whole-number exponents to denote powers of 10.

1. Complete the following chart.

$76 \times 10^4 =$	
$76 \times 10^3 =$	
$76 \times 10^2 =$	
$76 \times 10^1 =$	
$76 \div 10^1 =$	
$76 \div 10^2 =$	
$76 \div 10^3 =$	
$76 \div 10^4 =$	

2. What pattern did you notice when you multiplied by powers of 10 in the chart?

3. Is this pattern the same for dividing by powers of 10?
   Explain your answer.

4. Complete each number sentence.

   A. _____ $\times 10^2 = 3{,}200$

   B. _____ $\div 10^3 = 0.029$

   C. $3.5 \times$ _____ $= 35{,}000$

5. Write the missing power of ten.

   A. $89 \times$ _____ $= 89{,}000$

   B. $0.46 \times$ _____ $= 460$

   C. $619 \div$ _____ $= 0.619$

(Answers are on page 156.)

COMPARE DECIMALS

5.NBT.A.3 Read, write, and compare decimals to thousandths.

5.NBT.A.3.A Read and write decimals to thousandths using base-ten numerals, number names, and expanded form, e.g.,

$$347.392 = 3 \times 100 + 4 \times 10 + 7 \times 1 + 3 \times \left(\frac{1}{10}\right) + 9 \times \left(\frac{1}{100}\right) + 2 \times \left(\frac{1}{1000}\right).$$

For questions 1 and 2, let represent 1 whole, ▢ represent 1 tenth,

▬ represent 1 hundredth, and ▪ represent 1 thousandth.

1. How would 3.214 be shown with these blocks?

2. What decimal does the following representation show? _____

3. Write the decimal 563.463 in words, using place value names.

   Five _____ sixty-_____ and four _____ sixty- _____ _____

4. Write "eight hundred seventy-five and twenty-nine thousandths" in standard form (using numbers and symbols).

5. Write 24.658 in expanded form.

24.658 = _____ $\times$ _____ + ___ $\times$ _____ +

___ $\times$ _____ + ___ $\times$ _____ + ___ $\times$ _____

6. Write $5 \times 100 + 9 \times 10 + 8 \times 1 + 3 \times \dfrac{1}{10} + 6 \times \dfrac{1}{100} + 2 \times \dfrac{1}{1,000}$ in standard form (using numbers and symbols).

(Answers are on page 157.)

COMPARING DECIMALS BASED ON PLACE VALUE

1. Check all of the number sentences below that are true. Explain why or why not.

   ☐ 342.52 > 34.252 _____

   _____

   ☐ 6.325 > 32.65 _____

   _____

   ☐ 27.465 < 27.456 _____

   _____

   ☐ 218.45 = 218.450 _____

   _____

2. Create a number sentence using >, <, or = that shows:

   A. a number greater than 347.580.

   B. a number equal to 347.580, but with a different number of places.

   C. a number less than 347.580.

3. Fill in the blank with >, <, or = to make each number sentence a
true statement.

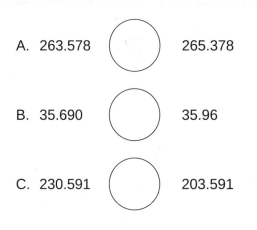

A. 263.578 ◯ 265.378

B. 35.690 ◯ 35.96

C. 230.591 ◯ 203.591

> When comparing
> decimals, it is helpful to
> write the numbers one
> below the other, with
> decimal points lined up.

4. Which statement is true?
  Ⓐ 35.97 < 35.964
  Ⓑ 647.31 < 647.310
  Ⓒ 45.28 > 4.528
  Ⓓ 82.456 > 82.46

(Answers are on page 157.)

ROUND DECIMALS

1. Use a number line to explain how to round 7.78 to the nearest tenth.

7.00   8.00

2. Use a number line to explain how to round 10.284 to the nearest hundredth.

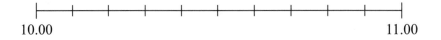

10.00   11.00

3. Explain how to round 5.5726 to the nearest thousandth.

_____

_____

_____

4. Round the following to the nearest tenth.

   A. 5.269   B. 34.783

5. Round the following to the nearest hundredth.

A. 269.572   B. 347.8342

6. Round the following to the nearest thousandth.

A. 62.3532   B. 345.7258

7. What is 2.47 rounded to the nearest tenth?
- (A) 3.0
- (B) 2.5
- (C) 2.4
- (D) 2.0

8. Which of the following would round to 7.6 when rounded to the nearest tenth?
- (A) 7.52
- (B) 7.56
- (C) 7.67
- (D) 7.69

9. What is 4.738 rounded to the nearest hundredth?
- (A) 4.7
- (B) 4.73
- (C) 4.74
- (D) 4.8

10. Select all answers that round to 6.34 when rounded to the nearest hundredth.
- ☐ 6.333
- ☐ 6.335
- ☐ 6.337
- ☐ 6.342
- ☐ 6.345
- ☐ 6.348

(Answers are on page 158.)

MULTIPLY WHOLE NUMBERS

5.NBT.B.5 Fluently multiply multi-digit whole numbers using the standard algorithm.

Calculate the answers to the following problems.

1.
$$
\begin{array}{r}
3,456 \\
\times \quad 6 \\
\hline
\end{array}
$$

2.
$$
\begin{array}{r}
83 \\
\times 47 \\
\hline
\end{array}
$$

3.
$$
\begin{array}{r}
549 \\
\times 76 \\
\hline
\end{array}
$$

4.
$$
\begin{array}{r}
270 \\
\times 85 \\
\hline
\end{array}
$$

5. Joey earned money this summer by mowing lawns and taking care of pets. He earned 14 times as much money this summer than he earned last summer. Last summer he earned $245. How much money did Joey earn this summer?

6. What is the product of 364 and 25?
   Ⓐ 8,800
   Ⓑ 8,900
   Ⓒ 9,000
   Ⓓ 9,100

7. What is the product of 3,160 and 7?
   Ⓐ 21,120
   Ⓑ 22,120
   Ⓒ 23,820
   Ⓓ 217,420

8. Lakeside Elementary School has 127 fifth graders. Each student turned
   in $45 for a field trip to the local amusement park. How much money
   was collected for the field trip?
   Ⓐ $5,715
   Ⓑ $4,715
   Ⓒ $4,385
   Ⓓ $1,143

9. The Moody Middle School cafeteria serves 625 lunches each day.
   How many lunches were served in March, if there were 21 school days
   in that month?
   Ⓐ 12,025 lunches
   Ⓑ 12,125 lunches
   Ⓒ 13,025 lunches
   Ⓓ 13,125 lunches

10. There are 5,280 feet in a mile. How many feet are in 15 miles?
    Ⓐ 31,680 feet
    Ⓑ 32,680 feet
    Ⓒ 77,800 feet
    Ⓓ 79,200 feet

(Answers are on page 159.)

DIVIDE WHOLE NUMBERS

5.NBT.B.6 Find whole-number quotients of whole numbers with up to four-digit dividends and two-digit divisors, using strategies based on place value, the properties of operations, and/or the relationship between multiplication and division. Illustrate and explain the calculation by using equations, rectangular arrays, and/or area models.

1. 350 ÷ 4 (Use the area model.)

2. 2,400 ÷ 5 (Use an array.)

3. 3,320 ÷ 8 (Use an equation.)

4. 9,235 ÷ 43 (Use the area model.)

5. Mrs. Jones bought a box of 64 markers to share among 4 groups of students. How many markers will each group get? (Array model)

6. If 98 pieces of poster board are shared equally among 15 classes, how many pieces will each class get? How many will be left over? (Equation model)

7. Southland School has 583 students. Each student will get a popsicle during field day. Popsicles come in boxes of 12. How many boxes will Southland School need? (Array model)

8. Six teachers shared a large box of paper equally. How many sheets of paper did each teacher get if 1,347 sheets of paper came in the box? (Equation model)

(Answers are on page 159.)

DECIMAL OPERATIONS

5.NBT.B.7 Add, subtract, multiply, and divide decimals to hundredths, using concrete models or drawings and strategies based on place value, properties of operations, and/or the relationship between addition and subtraction; relate the strategy to a written method and explain the reasoning used.

Use a place value chart to help in adding or subtracting these decimals.

1. 74.45 – 52.46

tens	ones	tenths	hundredths

2. 126.8 + 325.53

hundreds	tens	ones	tenths	hundredths

Use pictures, diagrams, and strategies you use with whole numbers to add, subtract, multiply, or divide. Use the space below to show how you solved each problem.

3. 33.25 × 5

4. 31.28 ÷ 4

5. 508.5 + .42

6. 204.03 – 98.6

7. Jessica added two decimal numbers that resulted in a sum of 76.23.
   What two addends could she have used? Justify your solution.

8. Travis was going to the beach, which was 284.8 miles away. After traveling 159.65 miles,
   how much farther did he have to go? Explain how you figured out the answer.

9. A tabletop measures 4.5 meters by 2.4 meters. What is the area in square meters?
   Use pictures, numbers, and words.

10. John bought a drink for $1.75 and a burger for $3.50. He has $17.50 left. How much did
    he start with? Show how you found your answer.

(Answers are on page 161.)

ADD AND SUBTRACT FRACTIONS

1. Use pictures to find equivalent fractions for the following:

    A. $\dfrac{3}{5}$ 　　　　　 B. $\dfrac{2}{7}$

Use equivalent fractions to add or subtract the fractions and mixed numbers below.

2. $\dfrac{3}{8} + \dfrac{1}{6} =$ 　　　　　 3. $\dfrac{4}{5} - \dfrac{1}{3} =$

4. $3\dfrac{5}{7} + 4\dfrac{1}{3} =$ 　　　　　 5. $5\dfrac{3}{4} - 2\dfrac{1}{6} =$

6. Katie lives $\frac{11}{12}$ of a mile from school. Angelo lives $\frac{1}{6}$ of a mile from school.

   How much closer to school does Angelo live than Katie?

   Ⓐ $\frac{1}{12}$ of a mile

   Ⓑ $\frac{3}{4}$ of a mile

   Ⓒ $\frac{7}{8}$ of a mile

   Ⓓ $\frac{10}{12}$ of a mile

7. Taylor ran $2\frac{1}{4}$ miles and walked $2\frac{4}{5}$ miles. How far did she run and walk altogether?

   Ⓐ 5 miles

   Ⓑ $5\frac{1}{20}$ miles

   Ⓒ $5\frac{1}{10}$ miles

   Ⓓ $5\frac{1}{2}$ miles

8. Madison used $8\frac{2}{3}$ cups white flour and $9\frac{1}{4}$ cups wheat flour to bake a cake.

   How many more cups of wheat flour than white flour did Madison use?

   Ⓐ $\frac{7}{12}$ cup

   Ⓑ $\frac{17}{24}$ cup

   Ⓒ $1\frac{3}{8}$ cup

   Ⓓ $1\frac{7}{12}$ cup

(Answers are on page 164.)

FRACTION WORD PROBLEMS: ADD AND SUBTRACT

5.NF.A.2 Solve word problems involving addition and subtraction of fractions referring to the same whole, including cases of unlike denominators, e.g., by using visual fraction models or equations to represent the problem. Use benchmark fractions and number sense of fractions to estimate mentally and assess the reasonableness of answers.

1. Carrie used $\frac{3}{8}$ yards of fabric to make curtains. She has $\frac{1}{4}$ yards left. How much fabric did she start with? Use pictures or equations to show how you found your answer.

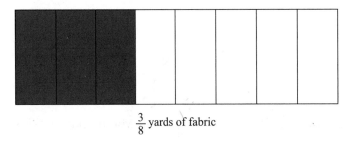

$\frac{3}{8}$ yards of fabric

2. Timmy completed $\frac{1}{5}$ of a puzzle. Jordan completed $\frac{2}{3}$ of the puzzle. How much of the whole puzzle have they completed? Use pictures or equations to show how you found your answer.

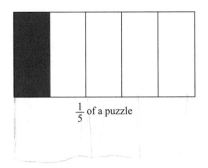

$\frac{1}{5}$ of a puzzle

3. Wanda was wrapping a gift for a birthday party, and she bought 4 yards of wrapping paper. After wrapping the gift, she had $1\frac{2}{5}$ yards of wrapping paper left. How much wrapping paper did she use? Show how you found your answer.

4 yards of wrapping paper

4. Kennedy bought $4\frac{1}{2}$ pounds of fudge at the fudge shop. She gave $1\frac{1}{8}$ pounds to her friend. How many pounds of fudge did Kennedy have left after giving some to her friend?

$4\frac{1}{2}$ pounds of fudge

5. Using estimation, state whether each sum is greater than or less than 1 whole. Explain your thinking.

A. $\frac{2}{5} + \frac{4}{9}$

_____

_____

B. $\frac{3}{5} + \frac{5}{7}$

_____

_____

6. Using estimation, state whether each difference is greater than or less than $\frac{1}{2}$. Explain your thinking.

A. $\frac{5}{6} - \frac{5}{9}$

_____

_____

B. $\frac{4}{5} - \frac{1}{10}$

_____

_____

7. On a math quiz, a friend stated that the answer to $\frac{1}{5} + \frac{3}{4}$ was $\frac{4}{9}$. Use what you know about adding fractions and reasonable answers to help your friend understand his mistake.

8. Jennie ran $\frac{3}{4}$ of a mile on Saturday and $\frac{5}{6}$ of a mile on Sunday.

   On which day did Jennie run farther? Explain how you know.

(Answers are on page 166.)

DIVIDE WHOLE NUMBERS AND FRACTIONS

5.NF.B.3 Interpret a fraction as division of the numerator by the denominator ($a/b = a \div b$). Solve word problems involving division of whole numbers leading to answers in the form of fractions or mixed numbers, e.g., by using visual fraction models or equations to represent the problem.

1. Mrs. Smith has 20 students and 12 candy bars. How much of a candy bar will each student get if Mrs. Smith gives each student an equal-sized piece?

2. At a birthday party, 16 people will share 4 large pizzas. How much of a pizza will each person get to eat? Use pictures, numbers, and words to show your answer.

3. Choose all of the situations below that have the solution $\frac{2}{3}$.

☐ A. The amount of rope licorice per person if 2 people share 3 feet of licorice equally.

☐ B. The part of a pie for each guest if 6 pies are shared equally among 9 guests at a party.

☐ C. The amount of the money each person gets if 8 people share $12 equally.

☐ D. The part of a big brownie each person gets if 4 brownies are shared equally by 6 people.

☐ E. The part of a relay race each person on a running team will run if 12 people share a 16-mile race equally.

☐ F. The part of an apartment each painter will paint if the painting of 8 apartments is shared equally by 12 painters.

4. There are 4 carpenters, each with $\frac{3}{4}$ of a sheet of plywood. How many sheets of plywood do they have all together?

   Ⓐ $\frac{3}{16}$ of a sheet of plywood   Ⓒ $3\frac{1}{4}$ sheets of plywood

   Ⓑ 3 sheets of plywood   Ⓓ $4\frac{3}{4}$ sheets of plywood

5. If 5 classes of fifth graders will share 42 liters of water, how many liters will each class get?

   Ⓐ 47 liters   Ⓒ $8\frac{2}{5}$ liters

   Ⓑ 37 liters   Ⓓ $\frac{5}{42}$ of a liter

6. A relay race runner runs $\frac{3}{10}$ of every mile. If the relay is 10 miles long, how far will she run?

   Ⓐ 3 miles   Ⓒ $10\frac{3}{10}$ miles

   Ⓑ $9\frac{7}{10}$ miles   Ⓓ 30 miles

7. Match each situation with the correct equation.

   ___ 1. 6 students share 40 cookies   A. $20 \div 3 = 6\frac{2}{3}$

   ___ 2. 6 boxes of ice cream shared by 40 people   B. $6 \div 40 = \frac{3}{20}$

   ___ 3. 3 packs of gum shared by 20 people   C. $40 \div 6 = 6\frac{2}{3}$

   ___ 4. 3 classes share 20 boxes of crayons   D. $3 \div 20 = \frac{3}{20}$

(Answers are on page 168.)

MULTIPLY WHOLE NUMBERS AND FRACTIONS

5.NF.B.4 Apply and extend previous understandings of multiplication to multiply a fraction or whole number by a fraction.

5.NF.B.4.A Interpret the product $(a/b) \times q$ as a parts of a partition of q into b equal parts; equivalently, as the result of a sequence of operations $a \times q \div b$.

5.NF.B.4.B Find the area of a rectangle with fractional side lengths by tiling it with unit squares of the appropriate unit fraction side lengths, and show that the area is the same as would be found by multiplying the side lengths. Multiply fractional side lengths to find areas of rectangles, and represent fraction products as rectangular areas.

Use the equation $\frac{3}{4} \times 3 = \frac{9}{4}$ for questions 1 and 2.

1. Create a story problem for this equation.

2. Using pictures as visual models, show that $\frac{3}{4} \times 3 = \frac{9}{4}$.

Use the equation $\frac{3}{4} \times \frac{3}{5} = \frac{9}{20}$ for questions 3 and 4.

3. Create a story problem for this equation.

4. Using pictures as visual models, show that $\frac{3}{4} \times \frac{3}{5} = \frac{9}{20}$.

5. Create a story problem for $\frac{2}{5} \times \frac{1}{3} = \frac{2}{15}$, then solve it using visual models.

6. What is the area of the rectangle below?

4 units

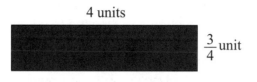

$\frac{3}{4}$ unit

7. Sara is making pillows. She must cut each piece of material into rectangles that measure $\frac{1}{4}$ of a yard wide and $\frac{2}{3}$ of a yard long. What is the area of each piece of material? Use the area model to show your answer in pictures, numbers, and words.

(Answers are on page 171.)

MULTIPLICATION AS SCALING

1. Shelly wants to make 5 pitchers of tea. Each pitcher needs $\frac{1}{4}$ cup of sugar. If she makes 5 pitchers of tea, will she have more or less than 1 whole cup of sugar? Explain your reasoning.

2. When Maria solved the problem $\frac{2}{3} \times \frac{1}{5}$ she got an answer of $\frac{2}{15}$. Jenny thought this answer was incorrect because she thought multiplication results in a product larger than the factors. Use what you know about multiplying fractions to explain why Maria's answer is correct.

3. Which statement is true about the product of $\frac{5}{8} \times 6$?

   Ⓐ The product is greater than each factor.

   Ⓑ The product is less than each factor.

   Ⓒ The product is greater than $\frac{5}{8}$ but less than 6.

   Ⓓ The product is equal to one of the factors.

4. Write an expression that will have a product less than both factors.

Explain how you know your expression is correct.

5. Write an expression that will have a product greater than both factors.

Draw a representation to show how you would simplify this expression.

Compare each pair of equations below. Explain which result is larger and which result is smaller and why.

6. 1×66 and $\frac{2}{3} \times 66$

7. $2\frac{1}{3} \times 23$ and $\frac{1}{3} \times 23$

8. $\frac{2}{3} \times \frac{3}{9}$ and $2 \times \frac{3}{9}$

9. $\frac{1}{6} \times 7$ and $1\frac{1}{6} \times 7$

10. $8\frac{1}{2} \times 2$ and $2\frac{1}{2} \times 8$

(Answers are on page 173.)

FRACTION WORD PROBLEMS: MULTIPLY

5.NF.B.6 Solve real world problems involving multiplication of fractions and mixed numbers, e.g., by using visual fraction models or equations to represent the problem.

Directions: Solve each problem below using pictures, numbers, and words.

1. Half of Delaney's bedroom is currently painted blue. She decided to repaint the blue walls with pink paint. At the end of the day, she had painted $\frac{5}{6}$ of the blue walls pink. How much of the whole room is now pink?

2. Joseph makes $12 per hour doing yard work. How much money does he make in $5\frac{1}{4}$ hours?

3. Jane uses $\frac{3}{4}$ of a cup of sugar for one gallon of iced tea. How much sugar does she need to make 3 gallons of iced tea?

4. Mrs. Klammer has a garden. One-half of her garden is planted in vegetables, and the other half is planted in flowers. She planted cucumbers in $\frac{1}{3}$ of the vegetable part of the garden. How much of the whole garden is planted in cucumbers?

5. Katelyn had $72. She spent one fourth of her money on a present for her sister. How much money did Katelyn spend?

6. A full grocery bag holds $5\frac{3}{4}$ pounds of goods. Jon carried 6 full shopping bags into his house in one trip. How many pounds did Jon carry in one trip?

7. Hannah has $\frac{3}{4}$ of a bag of candy left after a party. Today she ate half of what was left. What fraction of the bag of candy is left?

8. Taylor has a box of chocolates in which $\frac{3}{5}$ of the candies are milk chocolate. Of the milk chocolate candies, $\frac{1}{4}$ have caramel centers. What fraction of all the candies are milk chocolate with caramel centers?

9. Mrs. Riddell carried 7 boxes to her truck. Each box weighed $6\frac{3}{5}$ pounds. How much do all of the boxes weigh together?

(Answers are on page 175.)

FRACTION WORD PROBLEMS: DIVIDE

5.NF.B.7 Apply and extend previous understandings of division to divide unit fractions by whole numbers and whole numbers by unit fractions.

5.NF.B.7.A Interpret division of a unit fraction by a non-zero whole number, and compute such quotients.

5.NF.B.7.B Interpret division of a whole number by a unit fraction, and compute such quotients.

5.NF.B.7.C Solve real world problems involving division of unit fractions by non-zero whole numbers and division of whole numbers by unit fractions, e.g., by using visual fraction models and equations to represent the problem.

1. Create a story for $\frac{1}{3} \div 5$. Draw a visual fraction model to show how to find a solution.

2. Create a story for $\frac{1}{6} \div 6$. Draw a visual fraction model to show how to find a solution.

3. Create a story for $5 \div \frac{1}{8}$. Draw a visual fraction model to show how to find a solution.

4. Create a story for $7 \div \frac{1}{6}$. Draw a visual representation to show how to find a solution.

Directions: For each problem below, write an equation, and solve the equation using pictures, numbers, and words.

5. Laney wants to sew a pillowcase. If $\frac{1}{6}$ of a yard of fabric makes 2 pillowcases, how many yards of fabric does she need to make one pillowcase?

6. Marie is making oatmeal raisin cookies. She has 6 pounds of raisins. She needs $\frac{1}{4}$ of a pound of raisins to make one tray of cookies. How many trays of oatmeal raisin cookies can she make?

7. There are 24 pizzas for the lacrosse team's party at the end of the season. Each person can have $\frac{1}{3}$ of a pizza. How many people can be fed from the 24 pizzas?

8. Each relay race team will run a total of 3 miles. Each member of a team will run $\frac{1}{8}$ of a mile. How many people will each team need?

(Answers are on page 178.)

MEASUREMENT CONVERSIONS

Equivalent Measures

Type of Measure	Customary	Metric
Length	1 yard = 3 feet 1 foot = 12 inches	1 kilometer = 1,000 meters 1 meter = 1,000 centimeters 1 centimeter = 10 millimeters
Capacity	1 gallon = 4 quarts 1 quart = 2 pints 1 pint = 2 cups 1 cup = 8 ounces (oz.)	1 liter (L) = 1,000 milliliters (mL)

1. Jon's height is 2 yards, 2 inches. Joseph's height is 73 inches. Robert's height is 5 feet, 8 inches. Who is the tallest?

2. Sadie's backyard has a fence with 2 meters between posts. If the fence is 0.1 kilometers long, how many sections are there?

3. A sweet tea recipe calls for $\frac{1}{2}$ gallon of brewed tea, one quart of lemonade, and one pint of orange juice. How many cups (8 fluid ounces) of sweet tea will this make?

4. Madison has 8.4 liters of lemonade to serve 30 people. How many milliliters should she pour into each glass?

5. In the school Olympics, Kim threw the shot put 51 inches, Danielle threw it 4 feet 4 inches, and Megan threw it 1 yard, 1 foot, 1 inch. Who threw the shot put the farthest?

6. Samantha's hallway rug is 8 meters long and 75 centimeters wide. What is the area of her rug in square centimeters?

7. It took Amanda $3\frac{1}{4}$ hours to complete her project. Marla spent 230 minutes on her project. How much more time did Marla spend on the project than Amanda?

8. A red cooler holds 1 gallon, 1 quart, and 3 pints of water. A blue cooler holds 7 quarts and 5 pints of water. If each glass holds 1 pint of water, how many glasses of water can be served from these coolers?

(Answers are on page 179.)

LINE PLOTS

5.MD.B.2 Make a line plot to display a data set of measurements in fractions of a unit (1/2, 1/4, 1/8). Use operations on fractions for this grade to solve problems involving information presented in line plots.

Nine students had a contest to see who could jump on one foot the farthest. The table below displays the data from their jumps.

Blaine $1\frac{1}{4}$ feet	Kavon $1\frac{1}{8}$ feet	Noah 2 feet
Denny 2 feet	Davionna $1\frac{1}{4}$ feet	Savannah $1\frac{1}{4}$ feet
Christen $1\frac{1}{2}$ feet	Madison $1\frac{1}{2}$ feet	Angelo $1\frac{3}{4}$ feet

1. Create a line plot using the data.

1 foot   2 feet

2. What is the difference between the longest and shortest distance?

3. What is the total of the three shortest jumps?

4. Blaine, Davionna, and Savannah each jumped the same distance. Which equation would give the total of these distances?

    Ⓐ $3 \times 1\frac{1}{4}$

    Ⓑ $3 \div 1\frac{1}{4}$

    Ⓒ $3 + 1\frac{1}{4}$

    Ⓓ $3 - 1\frac{1}{4}$

5. The 4 girls (Christen, Madison, Davionna, and Savannah) jumped a total of $5\frac{1}{2}$ feet.

    If each girl had jumped the same distance, how far would that jump be?

Each person on the swim team was timed to see how long it took to swim the length of the pool. Below is a line plot that shows what fraction of a minute each person swam.

```
                          X
                          X
                          X
                          X
          X               X                           X                    X
          X               X                           X                    X
          X               X               X           X                    X
          X               X               X           X                    X
          X               X               X           X                    X
      <---|-------|---------------|---------------|-------|--------->
         1/8     1/4             1/2             3/4     7/8
```

6. How many people were timed? If the average time to swim a pool length were half a minute, what is the amount of time it would take all the swimmers to complete a relay if they swam relay style, one after the other?

7. A relay has a 5-minute time limit. How many quarter-minute swimmers would be needed to complete the relay?

The students in Mrs. Brennan's class measured their erasers in eighths of an inch. Below are the measurements of each student's eraser length.

$\frac{1}{2}$ $\frac{1}{8}$ $\frac{1}{4}$ $\frac{1}{8}$ $\frac{2}{8}$ $\frac{1}{8}$ $\frac{4}{8}$ $\frac{1}{8}$ $\frac{1}{2}$ $\frac{1}{4}$ $\frac{2}{8}$ $\frac{1}{8}$ $\frac{4}{8}$ $\frac{1}{8}$ $\frac{1}{8}$ $\frac{1}{2}$

8. Create a line plot based on this data.

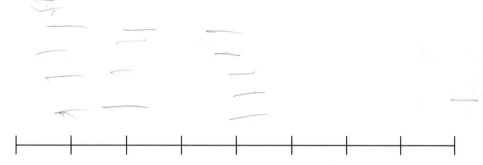

(Answers are on page 181.)

UNDERSTAND AND MEASURE VOLUME

1. If each edge of this cube measures 1 unit, what is the volume of this cube?

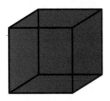

2. What is volume? How can you find the volume of a solid figure?

3. Jimmy has a new cube puzzle and is wondering how many cubes are used to make this puzzle. How many cubes are in this puzzle? Explain how you know.

4. If each cube measures 1 cubic cm, what is the volume of the figure below?

5. Each unit cube in this figure measures 1 cubic inch. What is the volume
    of this figure?

6. If each cubic unit in this box measures 1 cubic foot, how many cubic feet make
    the volume of the box?

7. What is the volume of this tower if each unit cube is 1 cubic meter?

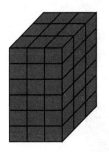

8. What is the volume of this figure in cubic units?

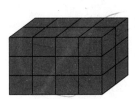

(Answers are on page 183.)

SOLVE VOLUME PROBLEMS

5.MD.C.5 Relate volume to the operations of multiplication and addition and solve real world and mathematical problems involving volume.

5.MD.C.5.A Find the volume of a right rectangular prism with whole-number side lengths by packing it with unit cubes, and show that the volume is the same as would be found by multiplying the edge lengths, equivalently by multiplying the height by the area of the base. Represent threefold whole-number products as volumes, e.g., to represent the associative property of multiplication.

5.MD.C.5.B Apply the formulas $V = l \times w \times h$ and $V = b \times h$ for rectangular prisms to find volumes of right rectangular prisms with whole-number edge lengths in the context of solving real world and mathematical problems.

5.MD.C.5.C Recognize volume as additive. Find volumes of solid figures composed of two non-overlapping right rectangular prisms by adding the volumes of the non-overlapping parts, applying this technique to solve real world problems.

1. Find the volume of cube *A*. How does the volume of cube *A* compare to the volume of cube *B*, which has a length of 3 cubic units, width of 3 cubic units, and height of 3 cubic units?

A　　　　　　　　　　　　　　　　　　　*B*

Volume of cube A = _____ cubic units　　Volume of cube B = _____ cubic units
(Each cube is equal to 1 unit.)

2. Compare the volumes of each of these rectangular prisms. Explain how you found the volume of each one.

3. A. If you are given the length, width, and height of a rectangular prism, how do you find the volume?

    Volume = _____

    B. If you are given the area of the base and the height of a rectangular prism, how do you find the volume?

    Volume = _____

4. What is the volume of this rectangular prism?

    _____ cubic meters

    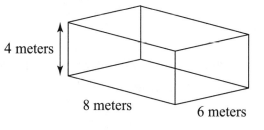

    4 meters

    8 meters

    6 meters

    Explain how you found the answer.

5. A wardrobe is 8 feet high with a base that has an area of 12 square feet. What is the volume of the wardrobe?

6. The volume of a rectangular prism is 72 cubic units. If the length of the prism is 6 units, what might the width and height be? How many possible solutions can you find?

7. A candy box is in the shape of a rectangular prism with the dimensions below.

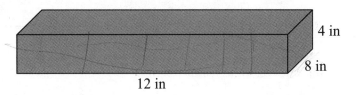

4 in

8 in

12 in

What is the volume of the candy box? Use words and numbers to explain how you got your answer.

8. The candy in the box is cut into 2 inch by 2 inch by 2 inch cubes. What is the greatest number of pieces that can fit in the candy box? Use words and numbers to explain how you got your answer.

9. How would you use the formula for volume to compute the volume of this figure? (Each cube is equal to 1 unit.)

10. Use the formula for volume to compute the volume of this figure. Use words and numbers to explain your answer.

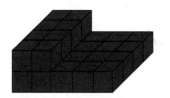

(Each cube is equal to 1 unit.)

(Answers are on page 184.)

UNDERSTAND THE COORDINATE PLANE

5.G.A.1 Use a pair of perpendicular number lines, called axes, to define a coordinate system, with the intersection of the lines (the origin) arranged to coincide with the 0 on each line and a given point in the plane located by using an ordered pair of numbers, called its coordinates. Understand that the first number indicates how far to travel from the origin in the direction of one axis, and the second number indicates how far to travel in the direction of the second axis, with the convention that the names of the two axes and the coordinates correspond (e.g., *x*-axis and *x*-coordinate, *y*-axis and *y*-coordinate).

Directions: Use the coordinate graph on the next page to complete the following tasks.

1. Label the *x*-axis and the *y*-axis, and label the origin (0, 0). Number each axis from 0 to 20.

2. Find the point at (3, 2). Label this point A.

3. Find the point (12, 7). Label this point B.

4. What is the ordered pair (*x*-coordinate, *y*-coordinate) for point C?

    (11, 10)

5. Describe how to find a point on a coordinate graph if you are given the ordered pair (6, 13).

    6 x axis   13 y axis

6. Describe how these two ordered pairs would be plotted differently.

    (3, 4), (4, 3)

    num pers are switchd axes

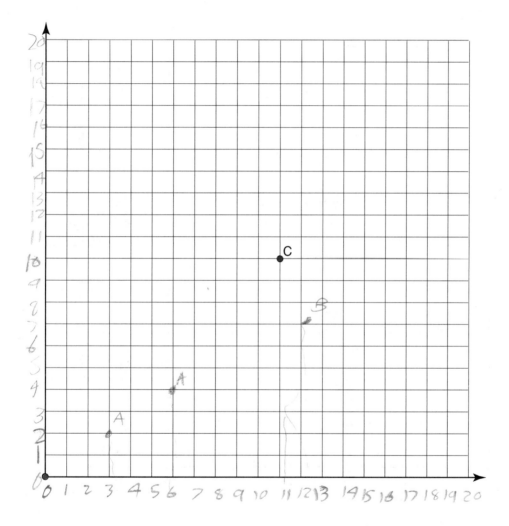

Directions: Use the graph below to create a coordinate system by completing the following tasks:

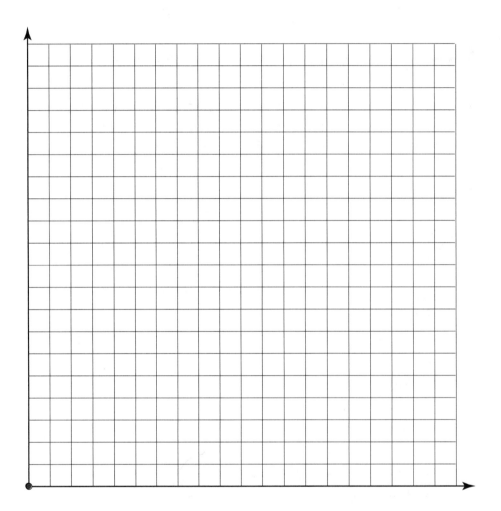

7. Label the *x*-axis and *y*-axis. Label the origin (0, 0). Number each axis starting at 0.

8. Draw the ordered pair (6, 4). Label it point A.

9. Draw 2 more points on your coordinate graph so that they form an angle when connected to point A. Label the points B and C. List the ordered pairs for these points:

   Point B: (_____, _____)   Point C: (_____, _____)

10. Connect points A, B, and C to form an angle. If you were to add 1 more point to make a parallelogram, what coordinates would you choose? List these coordinates for point D as an ordered pair:

    Point D: (_____, _____)

    Connect the segments to point D to make the parallelogram.

(Answers are on page 185.)

SOLVE COORDINATE PLANE PROBLEMS

5.G.A.2 Represent real world and mathematical problems by graphing points in the first quadrant of the coordinate plane, and interpret coordinate values of points in the context of the situation.

1. Savannah recorded the amount of rain and the high temperature each day for a week. Here are her results:

Day	Rain Total in Centimeters	High Temperature in F
Sunday	10	30
Monday	6	40
Tuesday	15	36
Wednesday	0	39
Thursday	10	35
Friday	14	38
Saturday	8	40

Graph this information as ordered pairs on the coordinate plane below.

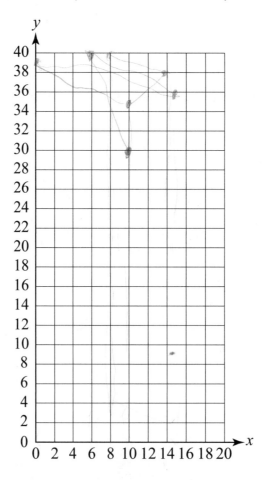

Use the coordinate plane below to answer questions 2 through 4.

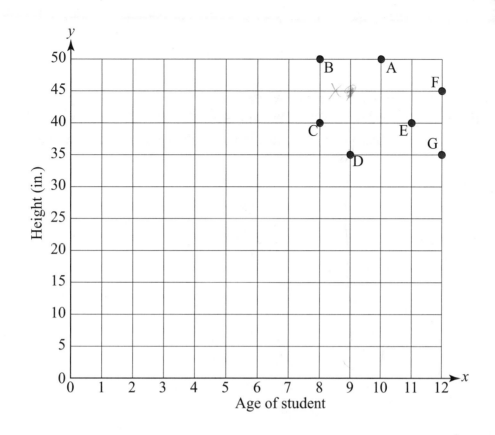

2. Mary is 50 inches tall and is 10 years old. Which point shows her characteristics?

   _____

3. Steve is 9 years old and 45 inches tall. His information is graphed incorrectly at point C. List the correct ordered pair for Steve's information and graph it correctly. Label this point X.

   (_____, _____)

4. Janna is unsure where to put her point. She is 40 inches tall and is 9 years old. Explain to Janna how to graph her information using an ordered pair.

5. Nikko and Joe are playing the game Battleship. Nikko calls the following ordered pairs: (4, 0), (5, 6), (8, 5), (2, 7), and (3, 9). For the last ordered pair, Joe stated, "Hit!" The battleship Nikko hit covers 5 points that are side by side on the grid.

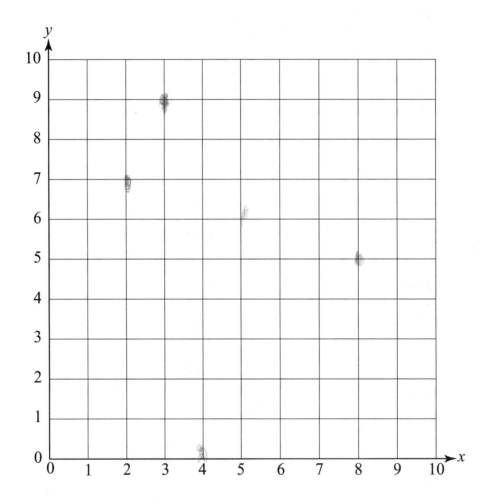

A. Graph the last ordered pair and 4 other ordered pairs that could be possible points that the battleship covered. Label the points A, B, C, D, and E.

B. List these ordered pairs:

A (_____, _____)   C (_____, _____)   E (_____, _____)

B (_____, _____)   D (_____, _____)

Use the following situation for problems 6 and 7.

Lisa swims 3 laps per minute in the pool.

6. Complete the chart, then graph the ordered pairs on the coordinate graph below.

Number of Minutes	Number of Laps	Ordered Pair
1	3	(1, 3)
2		
3		
4		
5		
6		

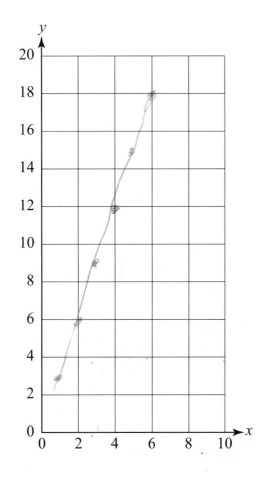

7. How many laps will Lisa swim in 10 minutes? In 20 minutes? What relationship do you notice between the *x*-coordinate and *y*-coordinate in each ordered pair?

Use the situation below to answer questions 8, 9, and 10.

Noah was using a coordinate plane to plan the arrangement of the furniture in his bedroom. In this grid, each square represents 1 square foot. Each piece of furniture in Noah's room is rectangular and will be positioned either horizontally or vertically. Noah's bed measures 7 feet by 3 feet. His desk is 3 feet by 5 feet. His dresser is 2 feet by 4 feet.

8. Use points and line segments to place the pieces of furniture onto the coordinate plane below.

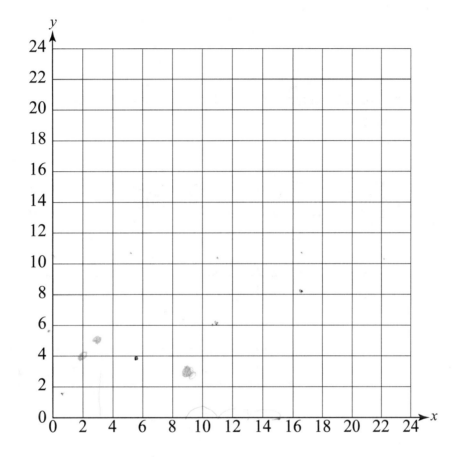

9. List the ordered pairs for each piece of furniture you placed on the grid.

Bed: _____   Desk: _____

Dresser: _____

10. What would the ordered pairs for the bed be if it were to be shifted 3 feet to the right along the x-axis?

(Answers are on page 187.)

UNDERSTAND ATTRIBUTES OF TWO-DIMENSIONAL FIGURES

> **5.G.B.3** Understand that attributes belonging to a category of two-dimensional figures also belong to all subcategories of that category. For example, all rectangles have four right angles and squares are rectangles, so all squares have four right angles.

1. Complete the chart below by putting an x in all the columns that apply to each two-dimensional figure.

Shape	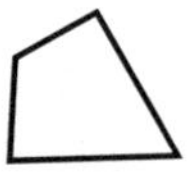	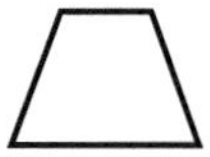			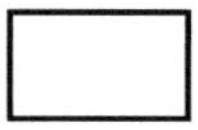	
Quadrilateral	•	•	•	•	•	•
Trapezoid		•				
Parallelogram			•		•	
Rhombus				•		
Rectangle					•	
Square						•

2. All squares are rectangles.

   True or False? _____

   Explain your answer using what you know about the attributes of squares and rectangles.

3. All squares are rhombuses.

True or False? _____

Explain your answer using what you know about the attributes of squares and rhombuses.

4. All parallelograms are rectangles.

True or False? _____

Explain your answer using what you know about the attributes of rectangles and parallelograms.

5. All trapezoids are quadrilaterals.

True or False? _____

Explain your answer using what you know about the attributes of trapezoids and quadrilaterals.

6. Which quadrilateral is described by the clues below? Name this shape, and draw an example.

This quadrilateral has 2 right angles.
One pair of opposite sides is parallel.
It has no congruent sides.

7. Which quadrilateral is described by the clues below? Name this shape, and draw an example.

   This shape has 2 pairs of parallel sides.
   All sides are congruent.
   It has no right angles.

8. Which quadrilateral is described by the clues below? Name this shape, and draw an example.

   This shape has 2 pairs of parallel sides.
   This shape has 2 pairs of congruent sides.
   It has at least 1 right angle.

9. Can a parallelogram also be a trapezoid? Why or why not?

10. You and a classmate are playing a game called Mystery Shape. You must turn your back and describe a quadrilateral you are thinking of without saying its name. She has all of the quadrilaterals in front of her. You want to describe the rhombus to her so that she will pick that shape and no other. How would you describe it to her?

(Answers are on page 189.)

CLASSIFY TWO-DIMENSIONAL FIGURES

5.G.B.4 Classify two-dimensional figures in a hierarchy based on properties.

Use the figures below to answer the questions. Each may be used more than once.

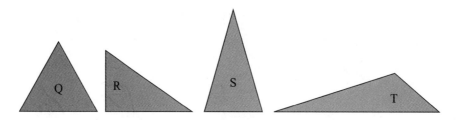

1. Which figure is an equilateral triangle?

    Explain how you know.

2. Which figure is an isosceles triangle?

    Explain how you know.

3. Which figures are scalene triangles?

    Explain how you know.

4. Which figure is a right triangle?

    Explain how you know.

5. Which 2 figures are acute triangles?

Explain how you know.

6. Which figure is an obtuse triangle?

Explain how you know.

You may use a ruler or protractor as aids to answer questions 7 through 10.

7. Circle all characteristics that describe this triangle:

right acute obtuse

scalene isosceles equilateral

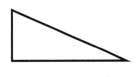

8. Circle all characteristics that describe this triangle:

right acute obtuse

scalene isosceles equilateral

9. Circle all words that define this shape:

quadrilateral trapezoid rhombus

parallelogram rectangle square

10. Circle all words that define this shape:

quadrilateral trapezoid rhombus

parallelogram rectangle square

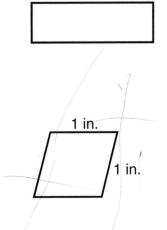

1 in.

1 in.

(Answers are on page 190.)

MATH
PRACTICE TEST

1. Which calculation should be done <u>first</u> to simplify this expression?

   $22 + 3 \times (10 - 4 \times 2) \div 2$

   Ⓐ 22 + 3
   Ⓑ 3×10
   Ⓒ 10 − 4
   Ⓓ 4×2

2. Evaluate the following expression.

   $55 \div (4 + 7) \times 6 + (15 \div 3)$

3. Which is a correct way of expressing $(6 + 9) \times (12 \div 4) - 3$?
   Ⓐ the sum of 6 and 9, times 12, divided by 4, minus 3
   Ⓑ 6 plus the product of 9 and 12, divided by the difference of 4 and 3
   Ⓒ the sum of 6 and 9, times the quotient of 12 and 4, minus 3
   Ⓓ 6 plus 9, times 12, divided by 4, minus 3

4. Write "the sum of the product of 7 and 12 and the quotient of 110 and 5" as a numerical expression.

5. Which set of ordered pairs has terms in one sequence that are 4 times the corresponding terms in the second sequence?
   Ⓐ (0, 0), (2, 8), (3, 12), (4, 16)
   Ⓑ (0, 4), (1, 5), (2, 6), (3, 7)
   Ⓒ (2, 6), (4, 8), (3, 10), (4, 12)
   Ⓓ (4, 16), (5, 17), (6, 18), (7, 19)

6. Which number is $\frac{1}{10}$ of 74?

Ⓐ 740
Ⓑ 7.4
Ⓒ 0.74
Ⓓ 0.074

7. Write the number that is 10 times as large as 0.48.

8. Match each number statement with the correct answer.

1. $58 \times \frac{1}{1,000} =$ A. 58

2. $58 \times 100 =$ B. 0.58

3. $58 \times \frac{1}{100} =$ C. 580

4. $58 \times 1 =$ D. 5.8

5. $58 \times \frac{1}{10} =$ E. 5,800

6. $58 \times 10 =$ F. 0.058

7. $58 \times 1,000 =$ G. 58,000

9. What power of 10 makes this number sentence true?

$0.29 \times$ _____ $= 290$

Ⓐ 10^1
Ⓑ 10^2
Ⓒ 10^3
Ⓓ 10^4

10. Write 47.295 in expanded form.

11. Write the decimal 346.729 in words, using place value names.

12. Which statement is true?
- Ⓐ 52.28 < 5.822
- Ⓑ 429.67 < 429.670
- Ⓒ 82.456 > 82.46
- Ⓓ 43.827 < 43.83

13. What is 5.47 rounded to the nearest tenth?
- Ⓐ 6.0
- Ⓑ 5.0
- Ⓒ 5.5
- Ⓓ 5.4

14. Select all answers that round to 8.54 when rounded to the nearest hundredth.

- ☐ 8.532
- ☐ 8.536
- ☐ 8.538
- ☐ 8.343
- ☐ 8.545
- ☐ 8.547

15. What is the product of 352 and 76?

16. There are 27 fifth graders in Mrs. Hall's class. Each student brought in 125 sheets of loose-leaf paper for the class. How many pieces of paper is this?
   Ⓐ 875 pieces of paper
   Ⓑ 1,125 pieces of paper
   Ⓒ 3,275 pieces of paper
   Ⓓ 3,375 pieces of paper

17. Find the quotient of 1,392 and 6.

18. Angela has a bag of 550 jellybeans, and she wants to share them with her 23 classmates. How many will Angela give to each classmate if she shares them equally? How many will be left over?

19. Tickets to a concert are $39.50 each. A group of 16 people are buying tickets. How much will tickets for the group cost all together?
   Ⓐ $44.50
   Ⓑ $23.50
   Ⓒ $632.00
   Ⓓ $6,320.00

20. Angelo won $250 in a contest. He went shopping and spent $72.45 of his winnings. How much money does he have left? Explain how you figured out the answer.

21. $\frac{3}{5} + \frac{4}{7} =$

22. $5\frac{1}{2} - 2\frac{1}{3} =$

    (A) $2\frac{1}{5}$ (B) $3\frac{1}{6}$ (C) $3\frac{2}{5}$ (D) $3\frac{13}{15}$

23. Sam ate $\frac{1}{6}$ of a candy bar. Jordan ate $\frac{1}{5}$ of the candy bar. How much of the candy bar did the boys eat? Is there more than $\frac{1}{2}$ or less than $\frac{1}{2}$ of the candy bar left? Use pictures or equations to show how you found your answer.

24. Sara has 10 yards of fabric to make a skirt. Her pattern uses $3\frac{5}{6}$ yards of fabric.

    After she makes the skirt, how much fabric will Sara have left? Show how you found your answer.

25. Choose all of the situations below that have the solution $\frac{3}{5}$.

    ☐ A. The amount of money each person gets if 9 people share $15.
    ☐ B. The part of a race each driver will drive if 12 racers split a 20-mile race.
    ☐ C. The part of a big brownie each person gets if 9 brownies are shared by 15 people.
    ☐ D. The amount of pizza per person if 10 pizzas are shared among 6 people.
    ☐ E. The part of a yard each worker will cut if 6 yards are cut by 10 workers.
    ☐ F. The amount of string per person if 3 people share 5 feet of string.

26. If 3 families will share 40 boxes of candy, how many boxes will each family get?

    (A) $\frac{3}{40}$ of a box of candy

    (B) $13\frac{1}{3}$ boxes of candy

    (C) 37 boxes of candy

    (D) 43 boxes of candy

27. Using pictures as visual models, show that $\frac{1}{3} \times \frac{2}{5} = \frac{2}{15}$.

28. The Smith family's garden is $\frac{4}{5}$ of a yard long and $\frac{3}{4}$ of a yard wide. What is the area of the Smith's garden? Draw a picture to help you solve this problem.

29. What is the area of a desk that measures $\frac{5}{8}$ of a meter by $\frac{2}{3}$ of a meter?

Ⓐ $\frac{3}{5}$ of a square meter

Ⓑ $\frac{7}{11}$ of a square meter

Ⓒ $\frac{15}{16}$ of a square meter

Ⓓ $\frac{10}{24}$ of a square meter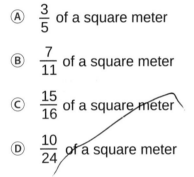

30. Which statement is true about the product of $\frac{5}{8} \times \frac{1}{2}$?

Ⓐ The product is greater than each factor.
Ⓑ The product is less than each factor.
Ⓒ The product is greater than $\frac{5}{8}$ but less than $\frac{1}{2}$.
Ⓓ The product is equal to one of the factors.

31. Which is larger? Explain how you know.

$\frac{2}{5} \times \frac{3}{8}$ or $2 \times \frac{3}{8}$

32. Solve using pictures, numbers, and words:

Sadie makes $7 per hour babysitting. How much will she make if she babysits for $6\frac{1}{2}$ hours?

33. Solve using pictures, numbers, and words:

Emily has $\frac{3}{4}$ of an apple pie left over from dinner. After lunch she ate half of what was left. What fraction of the pie is left?

34. Create a story for $4 \div \frac{1}{5}$. Draw a visual representation to show how to find a solution.

35. Charlotte has $\frac{2}{3}$ of a bottle of soda to split among 5 friends. What fraction of the bottle of soda will each friend get? Use pictures, numbers, and words to show how you solved this problem.

36. On field day, Breanna long jumped 62 inches, Myquisha jumped 5 feet 4 inches, and Ariana jumped 1 yard, 2 feet, 7 inches. Which list shows the girls in order from shortest to longest jump?

Ⓐ Breanna, Myquisha, Ariana

Ⓑ Myquisha, Ariana, Breanna

Ⓒ Ariana, Breanna, Myquisha

Ⓓ Breanna, Ariana, Myquisha

37. A limeade recipe calls for 1 gallon of water, 2 quarts of sweetened seltzer, and 1 pint of lime juice. How many cups (8 fluid ounces) of limeade will this make?

38. The table below shows the ages of 9 students in Mrs. Jefferson's class.

Wanneh	$10\frac{1}{4}$ years	Noah	$10\frac{1}{12}$ years	Blaine	$10\frac{2}{12}$ years
Kazia	$10\frac{1}{2}$ years	Zeb	$10\frac{5}{12}$ years	Savannah	$10\frac{1}{4}$ years
Niya	$10\frac{1}{6}$ years	Devon	$10\frac{3}{12}$ years	Travis	$10\frac{7}{12}$ years

Create a line plot using the data.

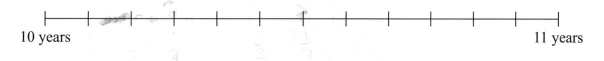

10 years   11 years

39. Use the line plot in question 38 to answer the following question.

What is the age difference between the oldest and youngest student in this group?

40. Define volume. How do you find the volume of a solid figure?

41. If each cube equals 1 unit, what is the volume of this figure?

_____ cubic units

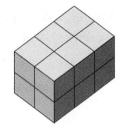

42. If each cube equals 1 unit, what is the volume of this figure?

_____ cubic units

43. What is the volume of this solid figure?

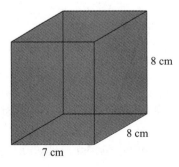

8 cm

8 cm

7 cm

- Ⓐ 23 cubic cm
- Ⓑ 64 cubic cm
- Ⓒ 71 cubic cm
- Ⓓ 448 cubic cm

44. What is the volume of a box that is 3 feet wide, 5 feet long, and 3 feet high?

45. If each cube equals 1 unit, how would you find the volume of this figure?

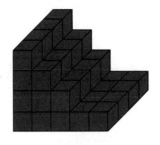

46. Graph and label the following ordered pairs on the coordinate graph below:

A (5, 3), B (0, 10), C (6, 7), and D (8, 5)

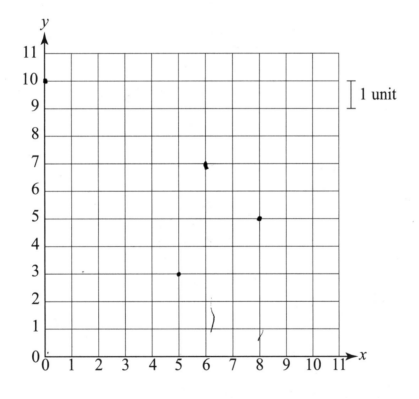

47. A square is a special geometric shape. Which other names also describe a square?

Check all that apply.

☐ Rectangle
☐ Rhombus
☐ Parallelogram
☐ Trapezoid
☐ Quadrilateral

48. Katie recorded the ages and heights of her family members. Here are her results:

Family Member	Age in Years	Height in Inches
Father	38	66"
Mother	35	62"
Older brother	15	60"
Katie	10	48"
Younger brother	8	42"
Younger sister	5	36"
Dog	3	15"

Graph this information as ordered pairs on the coordinate plane to the right.
Label each point as follows:

A—Father

B—Mother

C—Older brother

D—Katie

E—Younger brother

F—Younger sister

G—Dog

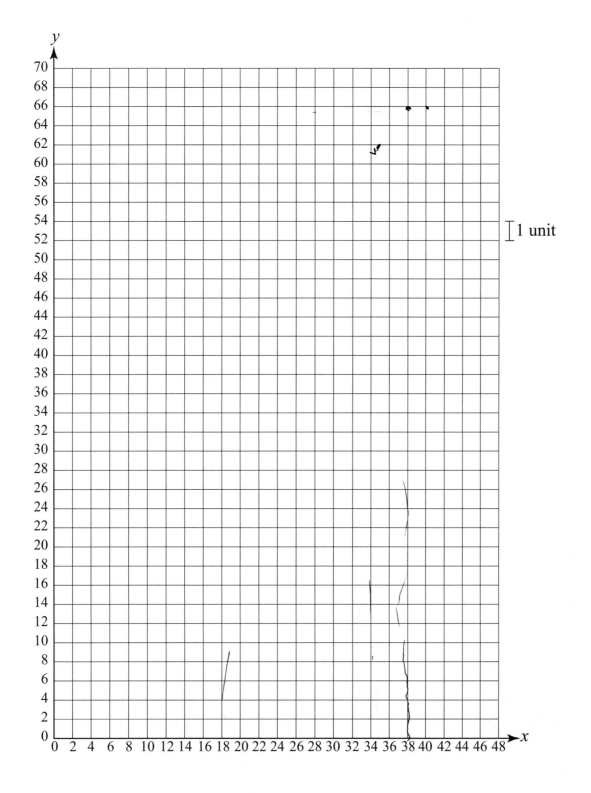

49. Which sentence best describes a rectangle?

Ⓐ A rectangle is a quadrilateral with 2 pairs of parallel sides.

Ⓑ A rectangle is a quadrilateral with 2 pairs of parallel sides and 4 right angles.

Ⓒ A rectangle is a quadrilateral with 2 pairs of parallel sides and 4 congruent sides.

Ⓓ A rectangle is a quadrilateral with 2 pairs of parallel sides and 4 noncongruent sides.

50. Which answer choice best describes this triangle?

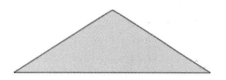

Ⓐ Acute and equilateral

Ⓑ Obtuse and equilateral

Ⓒ Acute and isosceles

Ⓓ Obtuse and isosceles

(Answers are on page 190.)

MATH ANSWERS EXPLAINED

OPERATIONS AND ALGEBRAIC THINKING

Evaluate Numerical Expressions, page 70

1. The order that operations should be carried out in evaluating expressions is as follows:

    1. Operations in parentheses should be carried out.

    2. Exponents should be worked out.

    3. Multiply or divide in the order the operations appear from left to right.

    4. Add or subtract in the order the operations appear from left to right.

    The steps to evaluate $20 - (3 \times 6) + (15 \div 5) \times 2$ are

     Step 1: Parentheses (3×6)
     Step 2: Parentheses $(15 \div 5)$
     Step 3: Multiply __ $\times 2$
     Step 4: Subtract $20 -$ __
     Step 5: ___ + ____

2.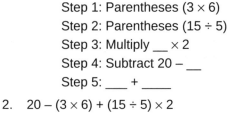
    $20 - (3 \times 6) + (15 \div 5) \times 2$
    $20 - 18 + (15 \div 5) \times 2$
    $20 - 18 + 3 \times 2$
    $20 - 18 + 6$
    $2 + 6 = 8$

3. **(C)** The operations in parentheses should be performed first. Thus, $(3 + 6)$ is the first calculation to perform.

4. Answers will vary. The situation must indicate that operations in parentheses occur first. For example, Madison needs 8 treat bags for her birthday party. Each bag will have 6 pieces of candy and 2 toys.

5. **(B)** First step: Operations inside brackets. $2 + 8 \times 6 - [(40 \div 5) - 1]$
    Inside the brackets, calculations inside parentheses should be completed first.

    $$(40 \div 5) - 1$$

    Next, subtract.

    $$8 - 1 = 7$$

    The expression now becomes $2 + 8 \times 6 - 7$.
    The next step is to multiply or divide from left to right.

    $$2 + 8 \times 6 - 7 = 2 + 48 - 7$$

    Next, add or subtract from left to right.

    $$2 + 48 - 7 \text{ or } 50 - 7 = \textbf{43}$$

6. **(C)** We first look for parentheses and other grouping symbols. Since there are none, we then multiply or divide in the order that they occur. In this expression, division appears first. So, multiplication of 10×3 is the second operation.

7. $2 \times (9 \div 3) + 2 \times 3$

8. $[(3 \times 15) + 4] \div 7$

    First complete operations within the brackets.

    $$(3 \times 15) + 4 = 45 + 4 = 49$$

    Next, divide $49 \div 7 = 7$. Each friend will get **7** pieces of gum.

9. **(B)** Start with parentheses. Next, multiply by 3. Finally, subtract that answer from 13.

$$13 - 3 \times (4 - 1)$$
$$13 - 3 \times 3$$
$$13 - 9$$
$$4$$

10. **(C)** Multiplication is the last operation to be performed because it is the only operation outside of the brackets. The first operation is addition because it is in parentheses inside the brackets. Division would be next, as it is performed before subtraction. The only remaining operation is multiplication.

Write and Interpret Numerical Expressions, page 72

1. $(6 + 4) \times (15 - 3)$

2. Answers may vary. However, it is important that adding 8 and 3 is the first step in evaluating the expression. Possible answers are "7 times the sum of 8 and 3, minus 4."

   "Add 8 and 3, then multiply by 7, then subtract 4."

   To check your work: Once you have written the expression in words, work backwards by writing the numerical expression. If your new numerical expression matches the original numerical expression, you can feel confident that your written expression is correct.

3. $8 \times (423 - 276)$

4. Possible answers: "The quotient of the sum of 54 and 30 and the number 12" and "54 plus 30, divided by 12."

5. **(C)** The subtraction step in parentheses must occur first. "3 times the difference of 534 and 216, plus 14" implies that the difference must be found before multiplying by 3, which is correct.

6. **(A)** In the expression, 27 and 36 should be added first, then divided by 9. "18 more than" indicates that after 27 is added to 36 and divided by 9, then 18 is added.

7. ☐ The sum of 13 and 35, multiplied by 8, then subtract 2.

   ☑ Add 13 and 35, subtract 8 and 2, then multiply the sum and difference.

   ☑ The product of the results when 13 is added to 35 and 2 is subtracted from 8.

   ☐ 13 plus 35, times 8, minus 2.

   ☑ Multiply the sum of 13 and 35 by the difference of 8 and 2.

   ☐ Add 13 to 35 multiplied by 8, then subtract 2.

   The correct expressions must indicate that addition and division are performed first. The sum and quotient should then be multiplied.

8. ☐ $6 \times 12 - 5 + 15 \div 3$

   ☐ $6 \times (12 - 5) + (15 \div 3)$

   ☑ $6 \times [(12 - 5) + (15 \div 3)]$

   ☑ $[(12 - 5) + (15 \div 3)] \times 6$

   The correct expressions must indicate that subtraction and division occur first, and that multiplication is the final step.

9. $(32 \times 15) \div (17 - 9)$

10. Answers will vary. The written expression should state that the subtraction and division steps occur first, the two multiplication steps occur next, and the addition step occurs last.

    Possible answer: "3 times the difference of 14 and 5, plus 2 times the quotient of 35 and 5."

1.

Rule	0	1	2	3	4	5
Add 2	2	3	4	5	6	7
Add 4	4	5	6	7	8	9

2. The relationship between the corresponding terms is that the second set of numbers is 2 more than the first set of numbers.

3. (2, 4), (3, 5), (4, 6), (5, 7), (6, 8), (7, 9)

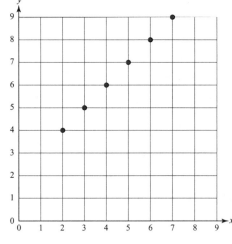

4.

N	N + 1	N + 5	Ordered Pair
0	1	5	(1, 5)
1	2	6	(2, 6)
2	3	7	(3, 7)
3	4	8	(4, 8)
4	5	9	(5, 9)
5	6	10	(6, 10)

5.

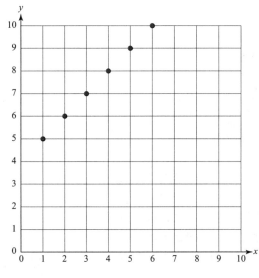

6. The relationship between the corresponding terms from the patterns of numbers generated in the chart in question 4 is that the second terms are 4 more than the first terms.

7.

N	N × 4	N × 2
0	0	0
1	4	2
2	8	4
3	12	6
4	16	8
5	20	10

The relationship between the lists of terms is the first term is twice the second term.

8. Ordered pairs: (0, 0), (4, 2), (8, 4), (12, 6), (16, 8), (20, 10)

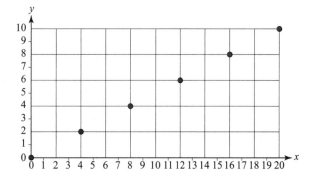

9. **(B)** Create a chart to determine the terms for each rule.

N	N + 2	N + 5
0	2	5
1	3	6
2	4	7
3	5	8
4	6	9
5	7	10

By examining the chart, it can be seen that the difference between 5 and 2 is 3, and the difference between 6 and 3 is also 3, and so on.

10. **(D)** By testing each set of ordered pairs, we find that 2 × 3 is 6, 4 × 3 is 12, and 6 × 3 is 18.

MATH ANSWERS EXPLAINED

1. Answers may vary. Important relationships between 123 and 1,230 include:

   "These numbers differ by one place" or "1,230 is 10 times larger than 123."

2. When comparing the underlined digits, the 3 in 43 represents 3 ones, whereas the 3 in 430 represents 3 tens.

3. When comparing the underlined digits, the 2 in 123 represents 2 tens, whereas the 2 in 1230 represents 2 hundreds.

4. When comparing the underlined digits, the 5 in 2.57 represents 5 tenths, and the 5 in 25.7 represents 5 ones.

5. A.

$43 \times 1,000$ (43×10^3)	43,000 (3 zeros)
43×100 (43×10^2)	4,300 (2 zeros)
43×10	430
43×1	43
$43 \div 10$	$\dfrac{43}{10} = 4\dfrac{3}{10}$ or 4.3 (1 decimal place)
$43 \div 100$	$\dfrac{43}{100}$ or .43 (2 decimal places)
$43 \div 1,000$	$\dfrac{43}{1,000}$ or .043 (3 decimal places)

B. Pattern: When 43 is multiplied by 1,000 or 100 or 10, the number of zeros in that factor are added to the end of 43. (1,000 has 3 zeros; 43,000 has 3 zeros.) When 43 is divided by 10, 100, or 1,000, the number of zeros in the power of 10 is the number of places in the quotient.

Multiply Powers of Ten, page 80

1. Explanations are included in parentheses.

$76 \times 10^4 =$	760,000 (4 zeros)
$76 \times 10^3 =$	76,000 (3 zeros)
$76 \times 10^2 =$	7,600 (2 zeros)
$76 \times 10^1 =$	760 (1 zero)
$76 \div 10^1 =$	7.6 (1 decimal place)
$76 \div 10^2 =$	.76 (2 decimal places)
$76 \div 10^3 =$	.076 (3 decimal places)
$76 \div 10^4 =$	.0076 (4 decimal places)

2. When a whole number is multiplied by a power of 10 (such as 10 or 100 or 1,000), the number of the power of 10 matches the number of zeros in the product. With decimals, the decimal point is moved to the RIGHT by the power of 10 because the product is that many times larger.

3. The pattern when a number is divided by a power of 10 is similar to multiplying by a power of 10. However, instead of adding zeros, the number of the power of 10 matches the number of places that

follow the decimal point. With decimals, the decimal point moves to the LEFT by the power of 10 because the quotient is that many times smaller.

4. A. ___32___ $\times 10^2$ = 3,200 (2 as exponent; 2 zeros because the product is 100 times larger)

   B. ___29___ $\div 10^3$ = 0.029 (3 as exponent; 3 decimal places left because the quotient is 1,000 times smaller)

   C. 3.5 $\times 10^4$ = 35,000 (4 as exponent; decimal moves 4 decimal places right because the product is 10,000 times larger)

5. A. 89 $\times 10^3$ = 89,000 (3 zeros because the product is 1,000 times larger)

   B. 0.46 $\times 10^3$ = 460 (decimal moves 3 places right because the product is 1,000 times larger)

   C. 619 $\div 10^3$ = 0.619 (decimal moves 3 places left because the quotient is 1,000 times smaller)

Compare Decimals, page 82

1. 3.214 would be represented by 3 wholes, 2 tenths, 1 hundredth, and 4 thousandths.

2. **2.423** The representation in this question shows 2 wholes, 4 tenths, 2 hundredths, and 3 thousandths. It is helpful to label each decimal place and then fill in the places:

$$\underset{\text{whole}}{\underline{\quad 2 \quad}} \cdot \underset{\text{tenths}}{\underline{\quad 4 \quad}} \quad \underset{\text{hundredths}}{\underline{\quad 2 \quad}} \quad \underset{\text{thousandths}}{\underline{\quad 3 \quad}}$$

3. In words, this decimal is read as "five hundred sixty-three and four hundred sixty-three thousandths."

4. The word form "eight hundred seventy-five" is written:

$$\underset{\text{hundreds}}{\underline{\quad 8 \quad}} \quad \underset{\text{tens}}{\underline{\quad 7 \quad}} \quad \underset{\text{whole}}{\underline{\quad 5 \quad}} \cdot \underset{\text{tenths}}{\underline{\quad\quad\quad}} \quad \underset{\text{hundredths}}{\underline{\quad\quad\quad}} \quad \underset{\text{thousandths}}{\underline{\quad\quad\quad}}$$

   The word form of the decimal "twenty-nine thousandths" means that there are 2 hundredths and 9 thousandths. (There are no tenths, so a 0 is placed in the tenths place.)

$$\underset{\text{hundreds}}{\underline{\quad 8 \quad}} \quad \underset{\text{tens}}{\underline{\quad 7 \quad}} \quad \underset{\text{whole}}{\underline{\quad 5 \quad}} \cdot \underset{\text{tenths}}{\underline{\quad 0 \quad}} \quad \underset{\text{hundredths}}{\underline{\quad 2 \quad}} \quad \underset{\text{thousandths}}{\underline{\quad 9 \quad}}$$

5. The decimal 24.658 has 2 tens (2 × 10), 4 ones (4 × 1), 6 tenths (6 × $\frac{1}{10}$), 5 hundredths (5 × $\frac{1}{100}$), and 8 thousandths (8 × $\frac{1}{1000}$). Putting this all together, 24.658 in expanded form is:

$$2 \times 10 + 4 \times 1 + 6 \times \frac{1}{10} + 5 \times \frac{1}{100} + 8 \times \frac{1}{1000}$$

6. Filling in the place value spaces, we have:

$$\underset{\text{hundreds}}{\underline{\quad 5 \quad}} \quad \underset{\text{tens}}{\underline{\quad 9 \quad}} \quad \underset{\text{whole}}{\underline{\quad 8 \quad}} \cdot \underset{\text{tenths}}{\underline{\quad 3 \quad}} \quad \underset{\text{hundredths}}{\underline{\quad 6 \quad}} \quad \underset{\text{thousandths}}{\underline{\quad 2 \quad}}$$

Comparing Decimals Based on Place Value, page 84

1. ☑ 342.52 > 34.252   342 is greater than 34.

   ☐ 6.325 > 32.65   6 is less than 32.

   ☐ 27.465 < 27.456   The whole numbers are equivalent. In comparing the decimals, 465 hundredths is greater than 456 hundredths.

   ☑ 218.45 = 218.450   The whole numbers are equivalent. In comparing the decimals, .45 has 4 tenths and 5 hundredths. Similarly, .450 also has 4 tenths and 5 hundredths. Both of these decimals also have no thousandths; therefore, they are equivalent.

2. Answers will vary. Sample answers:

A. 353.580 > 347.580   347.592 > 347.580   347.62 > 347.580

B. 347.580 = 347.58

C. 324.580 < 347.580   347.461 < 347.580   347.19 < 347.580

3. A. 263.578 (<) 265.378

B. 35.690 (<) 35.96

C. 230.591 (>) 203.591

4. **(C)** is true.   45.28 > 4.528   Looking at the whole numbers, 45 is greater than 4.

Round Decimals, page 86

1. On the number line, label each mark in hundredths—7.10, 7.20, 7.30, etc.

7.00	7.10	7.20	7.30	7.40	7.50	7.60	7.70	7.80	7.90	8.00

We know that 7.78 is between 7.70 and 7.80. If we mark where 7.75 is, we can see that 7.78 is closer to 7.80 than to 7.70. Thus, 7.78 when rounded to the nearest tenth rounds to 7.8.

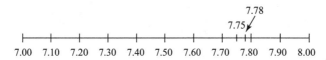

2. To round 10.284 to the nearest hundredth, underline the hundredth place.

1 0. 2 8 4

We know that 10.285 is between 10.280 and 10.290, so draw a part of a number line with these numbers as endpoints. Also mark the midpoint, 10.285.

If we place 10.284 on the number line, it will fall between 10.280 and 10.285, which is closer to 10.280 than 10.290. Thus, 10.284 when rounded to the nearest hundredth rounds to **10.28**.

3. We know that 5.5726 is between 5.5720 and 5.5730. Halfway between these two decimals is 5.5725. The number we are rounding, 5.5726, is greater than 5.5725, which means it is closer to 5.5730. Thus, 5.5726 rounded to the nearest thousandth is **5.573**.

4. A. 5.269 rounds to **5.3** because 5.269 is greater than 5.25, the halfway point between 5.2 and 5.3.

B. 34.783 rounds to **34.8** because it is greater than 34.75, the halfway point between 34.7 and 34.8.

5. A. 269.572 rounds to **269.57** because it is closer to 269.570 than 269.580.

B. 347.8342 rounds to **347.83** because it is closer to 347.830 than 347.840.

6. A. 62.3532 rounds to **62.353** because it is closer to 62.3530 than 62.3540.

B. 345.7258 rounds to **345.726** because it is closer to 345.7260 than 345.7250 (7,258 is closer to 7,260 than 7,250).

7. **(B)** 2.47 rounds to **2.5** because it is closer to 2.50 than 2.40.

8. **(B)** **7.56** rounds to 7.6 because it is closer to 7.60 than 7.50.

9. **(C)** 4.738 rounds to **4.74** because it is closer to 4.740 than 4.730.

10. ☐ 6.333

☑ 6.335

☑ 6.337

☑ 6.342

☐ 6.345

☐ 6.348

1. 20,736

2. 3,901

3. 41,724

4. 22,950

5.
$$\begin{array}{r} {}^{1}_{2} \\ 245 \\ \times\ 14 \\ \hline {}^{1} \\ 980 \\ {}^{1} \\ +\ 2450 \\ \hline \$\ 3{,}430 \end{array}$$

6. **(D)**
$$\begin{array}{r} {}^{1} \\ {}_{3}2 \\ 364 \\ \times\ 25 \\ \hline {}^{11} \\ 1820 \\ +\ 7280 \\ \hline 9{,}100 \end{array}$$

7. **(B)**
$$\begin{array}{r} {}^{1\ 4} \\ 3{,}160 \\ \times\ 7 \\ \hline 22{,}120 \end{array}$$

8. **(A)**
$$\begin{array}{r} {}^{1\ 2} \\ {}_{+3} \\ 127 \\ \times\ 45 \\ \hline {}^{1} \\ 635 \\ +\ 5080 \\ \hline \$5{,}715 \end{array}$$

9. **(D)**
$$\begin{array}{r} {}^{1} \\ 625 \\ \times\ 21 \\ \hline 625 \\ {}^{1} \\ +\ 12500 \\ \hline 13{,}125 \end{array}$$

10. **(D)**
$$\begin{array}{r} {}^{1\ 4} \\ 5{,}280 \\ \times\ 15 \\ \hline {}^{1} \\ 26400 \\ +\ 52800 \\ \hline 79{,}200 \end{array}$$

Divide Whole Numbers, page 90

1. 350 ÷ 4 (Area Model)

    A simpler problem for this is 35 ÷ 4. The closest multiplication fact to this is 4 × 8 = 32. Thus, we can use what we know about place value to use 4 × 80 = 320, shown with an area model.

    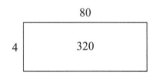

    We can then subtract 320 from 350.

    $$\begin{array}{r} 4\overline{)350} \\ 320\ (4\times80) \\ \hline 30 \end{array}$$

    With 30 left, a close fact is 4 × 7 = 28.

    $$\begin{array}{r} 4\overline{)350} \\ 320\ (4\times80) \\ \hline 30 \\ -28\ (4\times7) \\ \hline 2 \end{array}$$

    This can be shown using an area model:

    | 80 | + | 7 |

    $$\begin{array}{rr} 80 & 320 \\ +\ 7 & +\ 28 \\ \hline 87 & 348 \end{array}$$

    This model shows that 87 × 4 = 348. We have a difference of 2: 350 − 348 = 2. Thus, 350 ÷ 4 = 87 R 2.

2. 2,400 ÷ 5 (Array Model)

    In this problem, we know we will need 5 groups.

    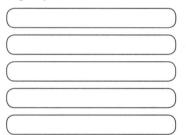

    Thinking of a simpler fact, we know that 5 × 4 = 20 is the closest that is less than 24. Using place value, then, we know 5 × 400 = 2,000.

    We can put 400 in each group.

    400
    400
    400
    400
    400

    We can then subtract 2,000, or 5 × 400, from 2,400.

    $$\begin{array}{r} 5\overline{)2{,}400} \\ 2{,}000 \\ \hline 400 \end{array}$$

We know that $5 \times 8 = 40$; thus, $5 \times 80 = 400$. We can put 80 in each group. Next, add what is in each group to find the answer.

400	80
400	80
400	80
400	80
400	80
2,000	400

$2,000 + 400 = 2,400$.

Thus, $2,400 \div 5 = 480$.

3. $3,320 \div 8$ (Using equations)

Equations can be helpful in estimating the answer before working out the exact answer.

Step 1: Write the division problem as an equation with a variable.

$3,320 \div 8 = n$

Step 2: Rewrite the equation as a multiplication problem using the multiplicative inverse.

$n \times 8 = 3,320$

Step 3: Round 3,320 to make compatible numbers.

$n \times 8 = 3,200$

8 and 3,200 are compatible numbers because $4 \times 8 = 32$.

Step 4: Estimate the answer.

$4 \times 8 = 32$, so $400 \times 8 = 3,200$

Thus, our estimate is that n = about 400.

We can then work out the problem and check our estimate.

$$
\begin{array}{r}
8\overline{)3,320} \\
3,200 \ (8 \times \underline{400}) \\
\hline
120 \\
-80 \ (8 \times \underline{10}) \\
\hline
40 \\
-40 \ (8 \times \underline{5}) \\
\hline
0
\end{array}
\qquad
\begin{array}{r}
400 \\
10 \\
+\ 5 \\
\hline
415
\end{array}
$$

Thus, $3,320 \div 8 = 415$, which is close to our estimate, 400.

4. $9,235 \div 43$ (Area Model)

Begin by creating a "Think Space" chart. Mentally multiplying 43 by 1, 2, 10, 20, 100, and 200 is quite simple (think zeros for place value!).

Think Space—Place Value

$43 \times 1 = 43$

$43 \times 2 = 86$

$43 \times 10 = 430$

$43 \times 20 = 860$

$43 \times 100 = 4,300$

$43 \times 200 = 8,600$

Draw a rectangle to represent the area model. Also, show the subtraction steps beside the rectangle.

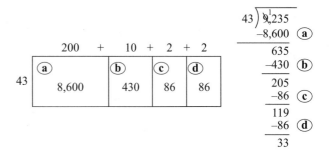

$200 + 10 + 2 + 2 = 214$. Thus, the answer is 214 R 33.

5. $64 \div 4$ (Array Model)

Make 4 rows.

10	6
10	6
10	6
10	6
40	24

$4 \times 10 = 40$, so we can put 10 in each row.

$64 - 40 = 24$

$24 \div 4 = 6$, so put 6 in each row. There are now 16 across each row.

We now have $40 + 24$, which is 64.

Thus, 64 markers $\div$ 4 groups = 16 markers per group.

6. $98 \div 15 = n$ (Equation Model)

$15 \times n = 98$

$15 \times n = 90$

$n \approx 6$

$$
\begin{array}{r}
6 \\
15\overline{)98} \\
-90 \\
\hline
8
\end{array}
$$

Thus, 98 pieces of poster board $\div$ 15 classes = 6 pieces per class, with 8 pieces left over.

7. (Array Model)

40	8
40	8
40	8
40	8
40	8
40	8
40	8
40	8
40	8
40	8
40	8
40	8
480	96

$$\begin{array}{r} 12\,\overline{)583} \\ -480 \quad (12 \times 40)\ \text{Step A} \\ \hline {}^{9}10\,3 \\ -96 \quad (12 \times \ \ 8)\ \text{Step B} \\ \hline 7 \end{array}$$

We must think about groups of 12. We know that $12 \times 4 = 48$ and $12 \times 5 = 60$. Similarly, $12 \times 40 = 480$ and $12 \times 50 = 600$. We will select $12 \times 40 = 480$, since it is closest to 583 without going over. Thus, draw 12 rows and put 40 on each row. Subtract 480 from 583.

(Step A)

There are 103 remaining. We know 12×8 = 96, which is close to 103. We can put 8 on each row and subtract 96 from our total. There are 7 left over.

(Step B)

Each row has 40 + 8, which is 48. Thus, 583 popsicles divided into boxes of 12 equals 48 R 7 boxes. The 7 remaining popsicles will come from another full box of 12. Therefore, Southland School will need 49 boxes of popsicles.

8. $1,347 \div 6 = n$ (Equation Model)

$$\begin{array}{r} 6\,\overline{)1,347} \\ -1,200 \quad (6 \times 200)\ \text{Step A} \\ \hline 147 \\ -120 \quad (6 \times 20) \\ \hline 27 \\ -24 \quad (6 \times 4) \\ \hline 3 \end{array}$$

Start with $6 \times n = 1,347$

A compatible number close to 1,347 that is divisible by 6 would be 1,200.

So $6 \times n = 1,200$

$n \approx 200$ (Step A)

After subtracting, we have $147 \div 6 = n$.

A compatible equation is $120 \div 6 = n$, with $n \approx 20$.

We then have 27 left over, or $27 \div 6 = n$. $24 \div 6 = n$ is more compatible, with $n \approx 4$.

We have $200 + 20 + 4 = 224$. Thus, each teacher will get 224 sheets of paper, with 3 left over.

Decimal Operations, page 92

1. $74.45 - 52.46$

tens	ones	tenths	hundredths
7	4 .	4	5
− 5	2 .	4	6

tens	ones	tenths	hundredths
7	${}^{3}4$.	${}^{13}4$	${}^{15}5$
− 5	2 .	4	6
2	1 .	9	9

(a) Fill in the decimals in the place value chart.

(b) Subtract as you would with whole numbers.

(c) Include the decimal in the solution so that we have the hundredths, since we added hundredths. (As a simple step, just bring down the decimal point.)

2. 126.8 + 325.53

hundreds	tens	ones	tenths	hundredths
1	2	6 .	8	0
+ 3	2	5 .	5	3

hundreds	tens	ones	tenths	hundredths
1	^{1}2	^{1}6 .	8	0
+ 3	2	5 .	5	3
4	**5**	**2 .**	**3**	**3**

After filling in the numbers in the chart, it is helpful to place a zero in the hundredths place for 126.8 (since .8 is equivalent to .80) so that hundredths are being added to hundredths. Next, add as usual and include the decimal point in your final answer to show hundredths.

3. 33.25×5 Think of this problem as "3,325 hundredths × 5." Our problem then becomes 3,325 × 5 (hundredths). We can then use strategies we use for whole numbers to multiply. For this problem, let's review the partial product method.

3,325 × 5 hundredths

x	3,000	300	20	5
5	15,000	1,500	100	25

Multiply to find partial products. Next, add the partial products.

```
 15,000
  1,500
    100
+    25
 16,625
```

FInally, place the decimal point so that the answer is in hundredths. **166.25**

4. $31.28 \div 4$ Think of this problem as "3,128 hundredths ÷ 4." Our problem then becomes 3,128 ÷ 4 (hundredths). We can then use strategies we use for whole numbers to divide.

For this problem, let's review the array method of division.

```
        2
   4)3128
   -2,800   (a)
      328
    - 320   (b)
        8
      - 8   (c)
        0
```

(a)	(b)	(c)
700	80	2
700	80	2
700	80	2
700	80	2

```
  700      80       2
×   4     × 4      ×4
2,800     320       8
 (a)      (b)      (c)
```

Divide using the array method (4 groups). We know 4 × 7 = 28, so 4 × 700 = 2,800. Distribute 700 to each group. Subtract 4 ×700, or 2,800, from 3,128, which is 328.

Next, 4 × 80 = 320, so distribute 70 to each group, and subtract 320 from 328, which is 8.

Then, since 4 × 2 = 8, put 2 in each group. We now have 782.

Lastly, place the decimal point so that the answer is in hundredths. **7.82**

5. 508.5 + .42 To add, we must make sure that we are adding the smallest decimal place values together; in this case, we are adding hundredths. Thus, 508.5 will become 508.50.

   Our problem then becomes 508.50 + .42.

   To add these numbers, we must line them up according to place value, and then we can add. Remember to include the decimal point so that the answer is in thousandths.

hundreds	tens	ones	tenths	hundredths
5	0	8.	5	0
+		0.	4	2
5	0	8.	9	2

6. 204.03 – 98.6 The smallest decimal place of these two numbers is hundredths; thus, adjust 98.6 so that it is in hundredths: 98.60.

   Next, line up the place values (line up the decimal points), and then subtract as usual.

   $$\begin{array}{r} {}^{1}2{}^{9}0{}^{13}4.{}^{1}03 \\ -\ 98.\,60 \\ \hline \mathbf{105.\,43} \end{array}$$

7. Answers may vary. Students must prove with addition that both numbers add up to 76.23.

   Solutions can be found by subtracting any number from 76.23. For example,

   $$\begin{array}{r} 76.23 \\ -\ 50.11 \\ \hline 26.12 \end{array}$$

   so 26.12 + 50.11 = 76.23.

8. $$\begin{array}{r} 2{}^{7}8{}^{14}4.{}^{7}8{}^{10}0 \\ -\ 159.65 \\ \hline 125.15 \end{array}$$

   Travis has **125.15** more miles to go to get to the beach.

9. **10.8 square meters** To find area, multiply length times width. One method to the solution is the area model. Rethink 4.5×2.4 as 45 tenths × 24 tenths. Then create an area chart.

	40	5
20	(20 x 40) 800	(20 x 5) 100
4	(4 x 40) 160	(4 x 5) 20

   Add the partial products: 800 + 100 + 160 + 20 = 1080

   Tenths × tenths = hundredths

   Thus, 45 tenths × 24 tenths = 1080 hundredths. Placing the decimal point so the answer is in hundredths results in the answer **10.80 square meters**. Applying what we know about equivalent decimals, 10.80 is equivalent to 10.8, since, for example, $0.80 can be shown with 8 dimes.

   To check reasonableness of our answer, 4.5 is about 5 meters, and 2.4 is about 2 meters, and $2 \times 5 = 10$. This is very close to 10.8, so our answer is reasonable.

10. To calculate what John spent on his drink and burger, add:

$ 1.75
+ 3.50
———
$ 5.25   John spent $5.25 on his meal

He still has $17.50. To figure out what he started with, add what he spent to what he still has:

$17.50
+ 5.25
———
$22.75   John started with **$22.75**.

Add and Subtract Fractions, page 94

1. Here are some examples of pictures that might be drawn to show equivalent fractions.

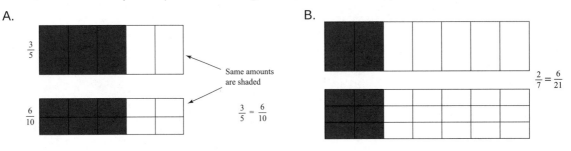

Computationally, to find equivalent fractions, the numerator and denominator must be multiplied or divided by the same number. (Answers may vary depending on which number is multiplied or divided.)

A. $\dfrac{3}{5} \times \dfrac{2}{2} = \dfrac{6}{10}$

B. $\dfrac{2}{7} \times \dfrac{3}{3} = \dfrac{6}{21}$

2. $\dfrac{13}{24}$

Step 1: Find the LCM (Least Common Multiple) of 8 and 6. List multiples of 8 and 6 until a common multiple is found.

8: 8, 16, *24*, 32

6: 6, 12, 18, *24*   LCM is 24.

Step 2: Rewrite the fractions as equivalent fractions with 24 as the denominator.

$\dfrac{3}{8}\boxed{\times 3} = \dfrac{\ }{24}$ 8 × 3 = 24, so the numerator must also be multiplied by 3.

$+\dfrac{1}{6}\boxed{\times 4} = \dfrac{\ }{24}$ 6 × 4 = 24, so the numerator must also be multiplied by 4.

$\dfrac{3}{8}\boxed{\times 3} = \dfrac{9}{24}$ Once equivalent fractions have been found with the same denominators,

$+\dfrac{1}{6}\boxed{\times 4} = \dfrac{4}{24}$ all that is left is to add the numerators.

$= \dfrac{13}{24}$

3. $\frac{7}{15}$ First, find the LCM of 5 and 3:

5: 5, 10, *15*, 20

3: 3, 6, 9, 12, *15*   LCM is 15.

Next, write equivalent fractions for $\frac{4}{5}$ and $\frac{1}{3}$ so that 15 is the common denominator. Last, subtract the numerators.

$$\frac{4}{5}\boxed{\begin{array}{c}\times 3\\ \times 3\end{array}} = \frac{12}{15}$$

$$-\frac{1}{3}\boxed{\begin{array}{c}\times 5\\ \times 5\end{array}} = \frac{5}{15}$$

$$= \frac{7}{15}$$

4. $8\frac{1}{21}$ First, find the LCM for 7 and 3:

7: 7, 14, *21*, 28

3: 3, 6, 9, 12, 15, 18, *21*   LCM is 21

Rewrite each fraction as equivalent fractions with the common denominator 21. Add the numerators.

$$3\frac{5}{7}\boxed{\begin{array}{c}\times 3\\ \times 3\end{array}} = 3\frac{15}{21}$$

$$+4\frac{1}{3}\boxed{\begin{array}{c}\times 7\\ \times 7\end{array}} = 4\frac{7}{21}$$

$$= 7\frac{22}{21} = 8\frac{1}{21}$$

5. $3\frac{7}{12}$ First, find the LCM of 4 and 6:

4: 4, 8, *12*, 16, 20, 24

6: 6, *12*, 18, 24   LCM is 12

$$5\frac{3}{4}\boxed{\begin{array}{c}\times 3\\ \times 3\end{array}} = 5\frac{9}{12}$$

$$-2\frac{1}{6}\boxed{\begin{array}{c}\times 2\\ \times 2\end{array}} = 2\frac{2}{12}$$

$$= 3\frac{7}{12}$$

6. **(B)** Find the GCF of 6 and 12. Since 6 is a factor of 12, and $6 \times 2 = 12$, the greatest common factor of 6 and 12 is 6.

$$\frac{11}{12}\boxed{\begin{array}{c}\times 1\\ \times 1\end{array}} = \frac{11}{12}$$

$$-\frac{1}{6}\boxed{\begin{array}{c}\times 2\\ \times 2\end{array}} = \frac{2}{12}$$

$$= \frac{9}{12} \text{ or } \frac{3}{4}$$

7.

$$2\frac{1}{4}\boxed{\begin{array}{c}\times 5\\ \times 5\end{array}} = 2\frac{5}{20}$$

$$+2\frac{4}{5}\boxed{\begin{array}{c}\times 4\\ \times 4\end{array}} = 2\frac{16}{20}$$

$$= 4\frac{21}{20}$$

$$4\frac{21}{20} = 4 + \frac{21}{20} = 4 + 1\frac{1}{20} = 5\frac{1}{20}.$$

8. **(A)**

$$9\frac{1}{4}\boxed{\begin{array}{c}\times 3\\ \times 3\end{array}} = 9\frac{3}{12}$$

$$-8\frac{2}{3}\boxed{\begin{array}{c}\times 4\\ \times 4\end{array}} = 8\frac{8}{12}$$

To subtract these fractions, we must regroup. 9 can be rewritten as 8 + 1, or $8 + \frac{12}{12}$. Thus, $9\frac{3}{12}$ becomes $8\frac{12}{12} + \frac{3}{12}$, which is equal to $8\frac{15}{12}$. Thus, $9\frac{3}{12} = 8\frac{15}{12}$.

$$8\frac{15}{12}$$

$$-8\frac{8}{12}$$

$$\frac{7}{12}$$

1. If Carrie used $\frac{3}{8}$ yards of fabric and has $\frac{1}{4}$ yards left, we must add to find out how much she started with. $\frac{3}{8} + \frac{1}{4}$

We can start by drawing $\frac{3}{8}$ of a whole.

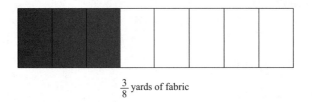

$\frac{3}{8}$ yards of fabric

Next, we can show the same whole divided into fourths.

We can see that $\frac{1}{4}$ is equivalent to $\frac{2}{8}$, so we can shade in $\frac{2}{8}$ on our drawing of a whole.

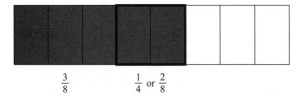

$\frac{3}{8}$ $\frac{1}{4}$ or $\frac{2}{8}$

We can see that $\frac{3}{8} + \frac{2}{8}$ (or $\frac{1}{4}$) $= \frac{5}{8}$. Thus, Carrie started with $\frac{5}{8}$ of a yard of fabric.

2. Our problem in this story is $\frac{1}{5} + \frac{2}{3}$. We can start by partitioning a rectangular puzzle into fifths and shading 1 piece.

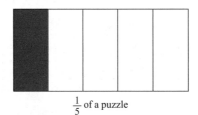

$\frac{1}{5}$ of a puzzle

Next, we can partition the puzzle into thirds, and outline 2 of those thirds.

1	2	3	4	5
6	7	8	9	10

Our puzzle is now subdivided into 15 pieces.

We see that $\frac{1}{5}$ is equivalent to $\frac{3}{15}$ and that $\frac{2}{3}$ is equivalent to $\frac{10}{15}$.

We can now arrange the pieces so that they do not overlap.

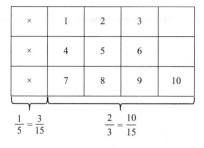

This diagram shows that $\frac{3}{15} + \frac{10}{15} = \frac{13}{15}$. Thus, **$\frac{13}{15}$** of the puzzle has been completed.

3. The equation for this word problem is $4 - 1\frac{2}{5}$.

To solve this, we can start by drawing 4 rectangles to represent 4 yards. We can also mark out 1 of those rectangles to represent 4 yards – 1 yard.

4 yards of wrapping paper

Next, we must subtract $\frac{2}{5}$. To do this, partition one of the rectangles into 5 sections, and cross out 2 of those sections.

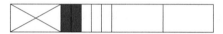

The remaining parts that are not marked off represent the amount of wrapping paper left.

We can see that 2 whole yards remain, as well as $\frac{3}{5}$ of a yard, for a total of $2\frac{3}{5}$ yards.

Thus, $4 - 1\frac{2}{5} = 2\frac{3}{5}$. Wanda used **$2\frac{3}{5}$** yards wrapping paper.

4. The equation for this word problem is $4\frac{1}{2} - 1\frac{1}{8}$. To solve this problem, we can start by drawing 5 whole rectangles to represent pounds of fudge and highlight $4\frac{1}{2}$ of those rectangles.

$4\frac{1}{2}$ pounds of fudge

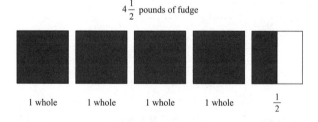

1 whole   1 whole   1 whole   1 whole $\frac{1}{2}$

Next, we must subtract $1\frac{1}{8}$. We can mark out 1 of the squares to represent 4 wholes – 1 whole.

We then need to subtract $\frac{1}{2} - \frac{1}{8}$. On the rectangle that shows $\frac{1}{2}$, we can partition that whole into 8 pieces, and cross off 1 of the shaded eighths.

We see that 3 whole rectangles are not crossed off, and $\frac{3}{8}$ of the shaded portion of the partitioned rectangle is not crossed off. Thus, $4\frac{1}{2} - 1\frac{1}{8} = 3\frac{3}{8}$. Kennedy has $3\frac{3}{8}$ pounds of fudge left.

5. A. $\frac{2}{5} + \frac{4}{9}$ Since each fraction is less than $\frac{1}{2}$ ($\frac{2.5}{5}$ is equal to $\frac{1}{2}$, and $\frac{4.5}{9}$ is equal to $\frac{1}{2}$), the sum will be **less** than 1 whole.

    B. $\frac{3}{5} + \frac{5}{7}$ Since $\frac{3}{5} > \frac{1}{2}$ (half of 5 is 2.5) and $\frac{5}{7} > \frac{1}{2}$ (half of 7 is 3.5), the sum of $\frac{3}{5}$ and $\frac{5}{7}$ will be **greater** than 1 whole.

6. A. $\frac{5}{6} - \frac{5}{9}$ $\frac{5}{6}$ is less than 1 whole and $\frac{5}{9}$ is more than $\frac{1}{2}$, so the difference will be **less** than $\frac{1}{2}$.

    B. $\frac{4}{5} - \frac{1}{10}$ $\frac{4}{5}$ is almost 1 whole, and $\frac{1}{10}$ is a very small piece of 1 whole. A fraction close to 1 whole minus a small piece of 1 whole will be **greater** than $\frac{1}{2}$.

7. $\frac{1}{5} + \frac{3}{4} = \frac{4}{9}$ is incorrect because $\frac{1}{5} + \frac{3}{4}$ will result in a sum close to 1 whole, and $\frac{4}{9}$ is less than $\frac{1}{2}$.

    Simply adding numerators and adding denominators will not result in correct answers.

8. To decide whether $\frac{3}{4}$ of a mile or $\frac{5}{6}$ of a mile is farther, we can think about the extra part of a mile that makes each fraction equal 1 whole. With $\frac{3}{4}$, we need one more fourth $\left(\frac{1}{4}\right)$ to make a whole mile. With $\frac{5}{6}$, we need one more sixth $\left(\frac{1}{6}\right)$ to make a whole mile. $\frac{1}{6}$ is a smaller piece than $\frac{1}{4}$; thus, $\frac{5}{6}$ is a bigger fraction than $\frac{3}{4}$. **Jennie ran farther on Sunday.**

Divide Whole Numbers and Fractions, page 100

1. $\frac{3}{5}$ **of a candy bar** To solve with pictures, draw a rectangle to represent 1 candy bar, and cut it into 20 pieces, 1 piece for each student. Shade in 1 piece to show how much each person would get from every candy bar.

Imagine having 12 candy bars just like this one. If 1 piece were shaded from each candy bar, we would have 12 small pieces.

However, if these 12 pieces were rearranged into a single candy bar, they might appear as $\frac{12}{20}$ of a candy bar:

or equivalently, $\frac{3}{5}$ of a candy bar.

Thus, each student would get $\frac{3}{5}$ of a candy bar. To solve with numbers, think of this problem as "12 candy bars divided among 20 students." 12 candy bars shared among 20 students = 12 ÷ 20, or $\frac{12}{20}$. $\frac{12}{20}$ can be simplified to $\frac{3}{5}$: $\frac{12}{20} \div \frac{4}{4} = \frac{3}{5}$

2. **Each person will get $\frac{1}{4}$ of a pizza.**

   (Responses in pictures, numbers, and words will vary. This is one possible way to represent the solution.)

   Draw 4 circles to represent 4 pizzas.

   Start evenly "slicing" each circle. One cut on each circle results in 8 even sections. One more cut on each circle will make 16 even sections.

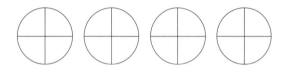

   There are now 16 pizza slices, enough for 1 slice for each party guest. Each person would get $\frac{1}{4}$ of a pizza.

   Thus, 4 pizzas divided among 16 people equals $\frac{1}{4}$ of a pizza per person. $4 \div 16 = \frac{1}{4}$

3. **B, D, and F**

   (B) 6 pies divided among 9 people would result in each person getting $\frac{2}{3}$ of a pie:

   $6 \div 9 = \frac{6}{9}$, which simplifies to $\frac{2}{3}$.

   (D) 4 brownies shared among 6 people would mean each person gets $\frac{2}{3}$ of a brownie:

   $4 \div 6 = \frac{4}{6}$, which simplifies to $\frac{2}{3}$.

   (F) 8 apartments shared by 12 painters means each painter paints $\frac{2}{3}$ of an apartment:

   $8 \div 12 = \frac{8}{12}$, which simplifies to $\frac{2}{3}$.

   (A) could not be a correct answer because 3 feet of licorice shared by two people would yield $1\frac{1}{2}$ feet of licorice per person: $3 \div 2 = \frac{2}{3}$ or $1\frac{1}{2}$

   (C) is incorrect because $12 shared among 8 people would result in each person getting $1\frac{1}{2}$ dollars: $12 \div 8 = \frac{12}{8}$, or $\frac{3}{2}$, which simplifies to $1\frac{1}{2}$ dollars per person. ($1.50)

   (E) is incorrect because 16 miles shared by 12 people means each person runs $1\frac{1}{3}$ miles. $16 \div 12 = \frac{16}{12}$, or $\frac{4}{3}$, which simplifies to $1\frac{1}{3}$ miles per person.

4. **(B)** To solve with pictures, draw 4 sheets of plywood, one for each carpenter. Because each carpenter has $\frac{3}{4}$ of a sheet, divide each sheet into 4 equal parts, and shade 3 parts of each.

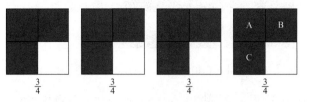

These parts can be rearranged to make whole sheets of plywood by moving sections of the last piece of plywood to fill in missing parts of the other 3 sheets.

We now have 3 whole sheets of plywood. Thus, 4 carpenters $\times \frac{3}{4}$ of sheets of plywood = 3 whole sheets of plywood.

$$\frac{3}{4} \times 4 = 3$$

To solve with numbers,

Method 1: $\frac{3}{4}$ of a sheet of plywood $\times$ 4 carpenters $= \frac{3}{4} + \frac{3}{4} + \frac{3}{4} + \frac{3}{4} = \frac{12}{4}$, which simplifies to 3.

Method 2: $\frac{3}{4} \times 4 = \frac{3}{4} \times \frac{4}{1} = \frac{12}{4}$, which simplifies to 3 when the numerator and denominator are divided by 4.

5. **(C)** 42 liters of water shared among 5 classes can be represented by $42 \div 5$, or $\frac{42}{5}$.

The improper fraction $\frac{42}{5}$ can be converted to a mixed number: 42 divided by 5 is 8, with 2 left over.

Our mixed number is $8\frac{2}{5}$.

$$42 \div 5 = \frac{42}{5} = 8\frac{2}{5}$$

Thus, 42 liters shared among 5 classes equals $8\frac{2}{5}$ liters of water for each class.

6. **(A)** A relay runner runs $\frac{3}{10}$ of every mile. The race is 10 miles long, which means she runs

$\frac{3}{10} + \frac{3}{10} + \frac{3}{10} + \frac{3}{10} + \frac{3}{10} + \frac{3}{10} + \frac{3}{10} + \frac{3}{10} + \frac{3}{10} + \frac{3}{10}$, which is equal to $\frac{30}{10}$, or 3 when simplified:

$30 \div 10 = 3$.

This can also be written as $\frac{3}{10} \times 10 = \frac{3}{10} \times \frac{10}{1} = \frac{30}{10} = 3$

Thus, the runner runs a total of 3 miles of the 10-mile relay race.

7. 1) C

2) B

3) D

4) A

1) "6 students share 40 cookies": This situation can be reworded, "40 cookies divided among 6 students" and can be represented by $40 \div 6 = 6\frac{2}{3}$.

2) "6 boxes of ice cream shared by 40 people": This situation means 6 boxes will be divided among 40 people. Symbolically, this is $6 \div 40 = \frac{6}{40} = \frac{3}{20}$.

3) "3 packs of gum shared by 20 people": This is 3 packs divided among 20 people, or $3 \div 20 = \frac{3}{20}$.

4) "3 classes share 20 boxes of crayons": This situation means 20 boxes will be divided among 3 classes, or $20 \div 3 = 6\frac{2}{3}$.

Multiply Whole Numbers and Fractions, page 102

1. Answers will vary. The story problem should involve having 3 wholes that are "sliced" into fourths, and then "taking" 3 parts of every whole.

    Here is an example problem: "A family ordered 3 pizzas. Three-fourths of each pizza was eaten. What fraction of the pizzas was eaten?"

2. A family ordered 3 pizzas. Draw 3 circles. If $\frac{3}{4}$ of each pizza was eaten, we need to first divide each pizza into fourths. We next need to mark off or shade 3 out of every 4 pieces, or $\frac{3}{4}$ of each pizza.

    We can see that 9 pieces are shaded in all. Each piece is $\frac{1}{4}$, which means there are 9 fourths shaded. Thus, $\frac{9}{4}$ of the pizzas were eaten. $\frac{9}{4}$ is equivalent to $2\frac{1}{4}$. Thus, $2\frac{1}{4}$ pizzas were eaten.

3. Answers will vary. The story problem should involve having $\frac{3}{5}$ of a whole and "taking" $\frac{3}{4}$ of that fraction.

    Here is an example problem: There is $\frac{3}{5}$ of a birthday cake left over after a party. The next day, $\frac{3}{4}$ of the left over cake is eaten. How much of the whole cake is left?

4. Show $\frac{3}{5}$ of a birthday cake shaded by subdividing a rectangle into fifths and shading 3 parts.

    Next, subdivide the rectangle horizontally into fourths, and shade in 3 of the fourths.

    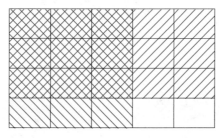

    We can see that 9 parts are shaded by both $\frac{3}{5}$ and $\frac{3}{4}$. We can also see that there are now 20 pieces of the rectangle. Thus, $\frac{9}{20}$ of the cake was left, which shows that $\frac{3}{4} \times \frac{3}{5} = \frac{9}{20}$.

5. Story problems will vary. Here is an example problem: One third of the lacrosse game has been played. Jon has been on the field for $\frac{2}{5}$ of the game so far. In how much of the game has Jon played?

    In this story, we might use a length model for our visual representation. Divide a line segment into thirds, and mark $\frac{1}{3}$ of the line segment to represent the part of the game that has been played.

    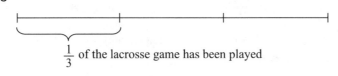

    $\frac{1}{3}$ of the lacrosse game has been played

    We now need to show $\frac{2}{5}$ of $\frac{1}{3}$. However, to clearly see the fractions in the problem, we need to subdivide each third into fifths.

    Next, mark $\frac{2}{5}$ of $\frac{1}{3}$.

    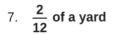

    We now see that the length model is partitioned into fifteenths. We see 2 of the fifteenths are marked. Thus, Jon has played $\frac{2}{15}$ of the lacrosse game so far.

    $$\frac{2}{5} \times \frac{1}{3} = \frac{2}{15}$$

6. $\frac{12}{4}$ **or 3 square units** Start by subdividing the rectangle into 4 parts vertically, and label each column "1". Next, subdivide it into 3 parts horizontally, and label each row "$\frac{1}{4}$".

    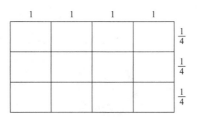

    We now see that there are 12 pieces, and each piece is $\frac{1}{4}$; so we have $\frac{12}{4}$. Thus, $4 \times \frac{3}{4} = \frac{12}{4}$.

7. $\frac{2}{12}$ **of a yard**

    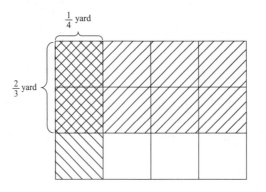

172

Subdivide a rectangle into fourths vertically, and shade in 1 column, or $\frac{1}{4}$ of the rectangle. Subdivide the rectangle into thirds horizontally, and shade in 2 rows, or $\frac{2}{3}$ of the rectangle.

We now have 12 sections, with 2 sections that overlap, or $\frac{2}{12}$. Thus, a $\frac{1}{4}$ yard by $\frac{2}{3}$ yard rectangle of material is equal to $\frac{2}{12}$ of a square yard.

$\frac{1}{4} \times \frac{2}{3} = \frac{2}{12}$.

Multiplication as Scaling, page 104

1. **More than 1 cup** Shelly would need $\frac{1}{4}$ of a cup of sugar for each pitcher, so she would be scooping sugar 5 times ($5 \times \frac{1}{4}$). One whole cup of sugar would be four scoops. Thus, Shelly would have **more than 1 cup** of sugar in 5 pitchers of tea.

2. Answers will vary. To understand the problem $\frac{2}{5} \times \frac{1}{5}$, it is helpful to consider $\frac{2}{3} \times 1$. We can think of $\frac{2}{3} \times 1$ as "$\frac{2}{3}$ of 1 whole," which we can show with a picture.

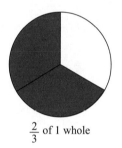

$\frac{2}{3}$ of 1 whole

We can see that $\frac{2}{3}$ of 1 whole is less than 1 whole; thus, in this situation, multiplication results in a product smaller than 1 whole.

Similarly, we can think of $\frac{2}{3} \times \frac{1}{5}$ as "$\frac{2}{3}$ of $\frac{1}{5}$". We can show this with a picture.

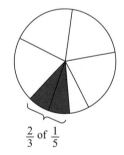

$\frac{2}{3}$ of $\frac{1}{5}$

We can see that $\frac{2}{3}$ of $\frac{1}{5}$ results in a fraction smaller than both $\frac{2}{3}$ and $\frac{1}{5}$. Thus, multiplying a number by a fraction results in a product smaller than at least one of the factors.

3. **(C)** The product is greater than $\frac{5}{8}$ but less than 6. We know that the product will be less than 6 because we are taking a fraction of 6. The product will be greater than $\frac{5}{8}$ because we will be taking $\frac{5}{8}$ of a whole, 6 times.

$\frac{5}{8} < \frac{5}{8} + \frac{5}{8} + \frac{5}{8} + \frac{5}{8} + \frac{5}{8} + \frac{5}{8} < 6$

4. Answers will vary. Correct answers should include fractions for both factors. Multiplying a fraction by a fraction results in a product less than both fractions because it means taking a smaller piece of a fraction of a whole. You could demonstrate this by drawing a picture. For example, $\frac{1}{2} \times \frac{1}{3}$ might look like this:

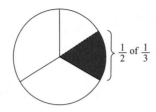

Taking half of $\frac{1}{3}$ produces a smaller piece than both $\frac{1}{2}$ and $\frac{1}{3}$.

5. Answers will vary. Correct answers should include at least one mixed number as a factor, as well as a whole number or a second mixed number as a factor.

An example expression might be $1\frac{1}{2} \times 3$. The drawing would show $1\frac{1}{2}$ three times. This drawing is more than $1\frac{1}{2}$ and more than 3.

6. 1×66 and $\frac{2}{3} \times 66$

$\frac{2}{3} \times 66$ is smaller than 1×66 because $\frac{2}{3}$ of 66 is only a fraction or piece of 66, while 1×66 results in 66 wholes.

7. $2\frac{1}{3} \times 23$ and $\frac{1}{3} \times 23$

$2\frac{1}{3} \times 23$ is a larger product because a picture of this expression would show 23 drawn 2 and $\frac{1}{3}$ times. $\frac{1}{3} \times 23$ would result in a smaller piece of 23.

8. $\frac{2}{3} \times \frac{3}{9}$ and $2 \times \frac{3}{9}$

$\frac{2}{3} \times \frac{3}{9}$ is a fractional piece of $\frac{3}{9}$. Conversely, $\frac{2}{3} \times \frac{3}{9}$ is $\frac{3}{9}$ drawn twice. Thus, $2 \times \frac{3}{9}$ is a larger amount.

9. $\frac{1}{6} \times 7$ and $1\frac{1}{6} \times 7$

$\frac{1}{6} \times 7$ is a fractional piece of 7. However, $1\frac{1}{6} \times 7$ is 1 whole group of 7 plus an additional $\frac{1}{6}$ of 7.

Thus, $1\frac{1}{6} \times 7$ is the larger product.

10. $8\frac{1}{2} \times 2$ and $2\frac{1}{2} \times 8$

$8\frac{1}{2} \times 2$ is $8\frac{1}{2}$ groups of 2, which can be broken down into 8 groups of 2 and $\frac{1}{2}$ of a group of 2, or 16 and 1, which equals 17. $2\frac{1}{2} \times 8$ can be broken down into 2 groups of 8 and $\frac{1}{2}$ a group of 8, or 4. This is 16 + 4, or 20. Thus, $2\frac{1}{2} \times 8$ is the larger amount.

1. In this problem, $\frac{5}{6}$ of half of the room is pink. This problem can be represented by the equation $\frac{5}{6} \times \frac{1}{2} = n$.

    First draw $\frac{1}{2}$ of a room. Then divide each half into sixths.

    Finally, shade in $\frac{5}{6}$ of one half.

    We have 5 pieces out of 12 shaded. Thus, $\frac{5}{6} \times \frac{1}{2} = \frac{5}{12}$. So $\frac{5}{12}$ of the whole room is pink.

2. **$63** $12 per hour for $5\frac{1}{4}$ hours translates to $12 \times 5\frac{1}{4}$. We can show this as repeated addition:

    $5\frac{1}{4} + 5\frac{1}{4} + 5\frac{1}{4} + 5\frac{1}{4} + 5\frac{1}{4} + 5\frac{1}{4} + 5\frac{1}{4} + 5\frac{1}{4} + 5\frac{1}{4} + 5\frac{1}{4} + 5\frac{1}{4} + 5\frac{1}{4}$.

    We have twelve 5s, which is 60. We also have twelve fourths. We can draw these fourths to find out how many whole dollars this is.

    We have $\frac{12}{4}$, which we see is 3 wholes. Putting the whole dollars and the fourths together, we now have 60 + 3, which is 63. Thus, $12 \times 5\frac{1}{4} = $63. Joseph makes $63 in $5\frac{1}{4}$ hours.

3. **$2\frac{1}{4}$ cups of sugar** $\frac{3}{4}$ of a cup of sugar per gallon × 3 gallons

    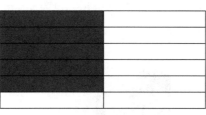

    These fourths can be rearranged to make wholes.

    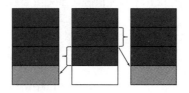

We are then left with 2 whole cups and $\frac{1}{4}$ of a cup.

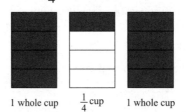

1 whole cup $\frac{1}{4}$ cup   1 whole cup

Thus, $\frac{3}{4} \times 3 = 2\frac{1}{4}$.

4. $\frac{1}{6}$ **of the garden.** Half of the garden is vegetables, and $\frac{1}{3}$ of the vegetable half is cucumbers. This translates to $\frac{1}{3}$ of $\frac{1}{2}$, or $\frac{1}{3} \times \frac{1}{2}$. This can be show in a drawing. First show half of a garden. Next, divide the halves into thirds. Shade in one of the thirds in one of the halves.

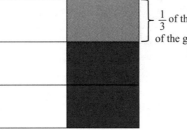

$\frac{1}{3}$ of the vegetable half of the garden is cucumbers.

We can see that of the whole garden, 1 of the 6 parts is shaded.

Thus, $\frac{1}{3} \times \frac{1}{2} = \frac{1}{6}$. **One sixth** of the garden is planted in cucumbers.

5.   **$18**   Katelyn spent $\frac{1}{4}$ of her $72 on her sister, or $\frac{1}{4} \times \$72$. We must partition $72 into fourths. We can do this by using the array model.

(a)   (b)

$15 $3

$15 $3

$15 $3

$15 $3

(a) Start by distributing $15 in each of 4 groups. We have $12 left.

(b) Distribute $12 by putting $3 in each group. There is now $18 ($15 + $3) in each group.

Thus, $\frac{1}{4}$ of $72 is $18, which is the amount of money Katelyn spent on her sister's present.

6. $34\frac{1}{2}$ **pounds**   Jon's 6 bags of groceries weigh $5\frac{3}{4}$ pounds each, or $6 \times 5\frac{3}{4}$. Using the Distributive Property, this breaks down into 6×5 and $6 \times \frac{3}{4}$.

$6 \times 5 = 30$

Draw 6 sets of $\frac{3}{4}$. Rearrange some of the fourths to make wholes.

We now have 4 wholes, with 2 fourths left.

Putting it all together, we have 30 pounds, plus $4\frac{1}{2}$ pounds, or $34\frac{1}{2}$ pounds.

Thus, $6 \times 5\frac{3}{4} = 34\frac{1}{2}$. Jon carried $34\frac{1}{2}$ pounds of groceries in 1 trip.

7. **$\frac{3}{8}$ of a bag** Hannah ate $\frac{1}{2}$ of the $\frac{3}{4}$ of a bag of candy, or $\frac{1}{2} \times \frac{3}{4}$. First draw $\frac{3}{4}$ of a bag.

Then divide that amount into halves, and shade one of the halves.

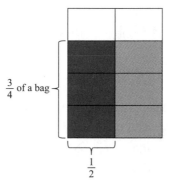

The bag of candy is now partitioned into eighths, and 3 of the eighths are shaded. Thus, $\frac{1}{2} \times \frac{3}{4} = \frac{3}{8}$. Hannah ate $\frac{1}{2}$ of the bag of candy.

8. **$\frac{3}{20}$ of a box** If $\frac{3}{5}$ of the candies are milk chocolate, and $\frac{1}{4}$ of those have caramel centers, we

would multiply $\frac{1}{4} \times \frac{3}{5}$. First partition the box into fifths, and shade in 3 of them. Then partition the

box into fourths, and shade in one of them.

There are now 20 pieces, and 3 of those pieces are shaded by both $\frac{3}{5}$ and $\frac{1}{4}$. Thus,

$\frac{1}{4} \times \frac{3}{5} = \frac{3}{20}$. Milk chocolates with caramel centers are in $\frac{3}{20}$ of the box of chocolates.

9. **$46\frac{1}{5}$ pounds** If each box weighs $6\frac{3}{5}$ pounds, and there are 7 boxes, this problem is $7 \times 6\frac{3}{5}$.

Using the Distributive Property, this is 7×6 and $7 \times \frac{3}{5}$. $7 \times 6 = 42$. A picture can be drawn to

show $7 \times \frac{3}{5}$. Draw $\frac{3}{5}$ seven times, and rearrange pieces to make wholes.

177

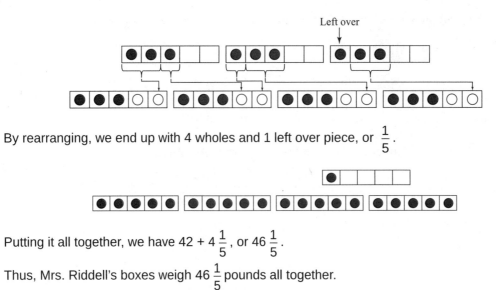

By rearranging, we end up with 4 wholes and 1 left over piece, or $\frac{1}{5}$.

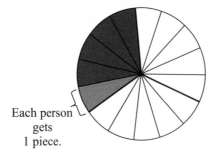

Putting it all together, we have $42 + 4\frac{1}{5}$, or $46\frac{1}{5}$.

Thus, Mrs. Riddell's boxes weigh $46\frac{1}{5}$ pounds all together.

Fraction Word Problems: Divide, page 108

1. Answers will vary. An example problem is: One third of a pie was left. Five people want to share it. What fraction of the whole pie will each person get?

   Draw a circle to represent the pie, partition it into thirds, and shade in one third to represent the third that was left. Subdivide each third into fifths.

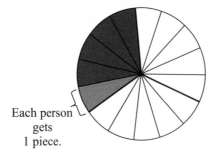

Each person gets 1 piece.

   There are now 15 pieces that make the whole pie. Of the shaded third, each person will get 1 piece, which is $\frac{1}{15}$ of the whole pie. Thus, $\frac{1}{3} \div 5 = \frac{1}{15}$.

2. Answers will vary. An example problem is: A piece of licorice $\frac{1}{6}$ of a yard long is being shared by 6 people. How much of the yard of licorice will each person get?

   This problem can be solved using a length model. Draw a line segment and partition it into sixths. Highlight one of the sixths to represent the piece of licorice being shared.

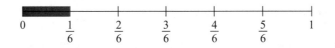

   Partition that piece into 6 pieces so that it can be shared. To determine what fraction each of those pieces represents, partition the rest of the unhighlighted pieces into sixths, as well.

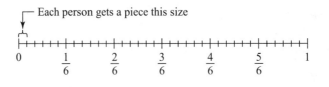

Each person gets a piece this size

There are now 36 pieces that make the whole. Each of the 6 people will get 1 piece of 36.

Thus, $\frac{1}{6} \div 6 = \frac{1}{36}$. Each person will get $\frac{1}{36}$ of a yard of licorice (which, by the way, equals 1 inch, since 36 inches equal 1 yard).

3. Answers will vary. An example problem is: There are 5 lasagnas that were baked for a party. Each guest will be served $\frac{1}{8}$ of a lasagna. How many guests can be served? This problem can be solved by drawing 5 rectangles to represent lasagnas. Partition each lasagna into eighths.

There are 40 pieces of lasagna, which means 40 guests can be served. Thus, $5 \div \frac{1}{8} = 40$.

4. Answers will vary. An example problem is: If 7 pizzas are ordered, and each pizza is cut into sixths, how many pieces of pizza will there be?

Solve this problem by drawing 7 circles to represent the pizzas, and subdivide each circle into sixths. There are 42 pieces of pizza.

Thus, $7 \div \frac{1}{6} = 42$.

5. $\frac{1}{12}$ **of a yard** This problem can be solved using a length model. Draw a line segment, partition it into sixths, and shade in one of the sixths. Partition the shaded sixth into 2 pieces to represent 2 pillowcases that can be made. To determine what fraction of the whole yard Laney needs to make one pillowcase, partition the rest of the sixths into 2 pieces each.

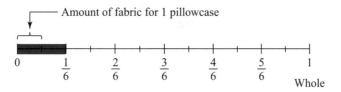

The whole yard is divided into 12 pieces. One pillowcase will require 1 piece out of 12, or $\frac{1}{12}$. Thus, $\frac{1}{6} \div 2 = \frac{1}{12}$. Laney needs $\frac{1}{12}$ of a yard of fabric to make 1 pillowcase.

6. **24 pans** Draw 6 rectangles to represent each pound of raisins, and partition each rectangle into fourths. There are 24 fourths, which means Marie can make 24 pans of cookies.

Thus, $6 \div \frac{1}{4} = 24$.

7. **72 people** Draw 24 circles to represent 24 pizzas, and partition each circle into thirds.

There are 72 thirds, which means 72 people can be fed pizza.

$24 \div \frac{1}{3} = 72$

8. **24 people** Draw 3 line segments to represent 3 miles, and partition each segment into eighths. There are a total of 24 eighths, which means 24 people must be on a relay team.

$3 \div \frac{1}{8} = 24$

Measurement Conversions, page 110

1. **Jon is the tallest.** To compare the heights of these 3 men, we must convert the heights into inches.

Jon's height: 74 inches
Joseph's height: 73 inches
Robert's height: 68 inches **Jon is the tallest.**

2. **50 sections**   We know that there are 1,000 meters in 1 kilometer. We need to figure out how many meters are in 0.1 kilometers.

$$\begin{array}{r} 1{,}000 \\ \times \quad 0.1 \\ \hline 100.0 \text{ meters} \end{array}$$

The fence is 100 meters long. If each section is 2 meters long, then 100 ÷ 2 = 50. Thus, Sadie's fence has 50 sections.

3. **14 cups**

Important equivalences:

8 ounces = 1 cup

2 cups = 1 pint

2 pints = 1 quart

2 quarts = $\frac{1}{2}$ gallon

Let's convert all of the measured beverages into ounces.

Thus, we have 64 ounces + 32 ounces + 16 ounces = 112 ounces (14 cups) of sweet tea.

4. **280 mL**   First, convert 8.4 liters to milliliters.

1 L = 1,000 mL

8.4 L = 8,400 mL

Next, to figure out how much to put in each of 30 glasses, divide 8,400 ÷ 30, which is 280. Thus, Madison will pour 280 mL of lemonade into each glass.

5. **Danielle threw the furthest**   In order to compare lengths, we can convert all 3 distances to inches.

Kim threw the shot put 51 inches.

Danielle threw it 52 inches.

Megan threw it 49 inches.

Danielle threw the shot put the farthest.

6. **60,000 square centimeters**   Samantha's hallway rug is 8 meters long and 75 centimeters wide. What is the area of her rug in square centimeters?

In order to find the area, we must convert 8 meters to centimeters:

1 m = 100 cm, so 8 m = 800 cm

Area = length × width, so we must multiply 800 cm × 75 cm.

$$\begin{array}{r} 800 \\ \times \quad 75 \\ \hline 4000 \\ +\ 56000 \\ \hline 60{,}000 \end{array}$$

Thus, the area of Samantha's rug is 60,000 square centimeters.

7. **35 minutes**   To compare the amount of time each girl took to complete the project, convert Amanda's time to minutes.

Amanda: 3 hours or 180 minutes

$\frac{1}{4}$ hour = 15 minutes, so 180 + 15 = 195 minutes.

Amanda spent 195 minutes on her project. Since Marla spent 230 minutes on her project, we can find the difference by subtracting 195 from 230.

$$230$$
$$-\ 195$$
$$35 \text{ minutes}$$

Thus, Marla spent 35 minutes more than Amanda on the project.

8. **40 glasses of water** Convert the amount of water in each cooler to pints.

Red cooler: 1 gallon, 1 quart, 3 pints

1 gallon = 4 quarts = 8 pints

1 quart = 2 pints

3 pints

16 + 2 + 3 = 21 pints (amount of water the red cooler holds)

Blue cooler: 7 quarts, 5 pints

7 quarts = 14 pints

14 pints + 5 pints = 19 pints (amount of water the blue cooler holds)

pints in red cooler + pints in blue cooler = 21 + 19 = 40 pints

Therefore, 40 glasses of water can be served from these two coolers.

Line Plots, page 112

1.

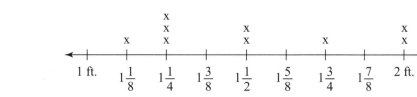

2. $\dfrac{7}{8}$ **of a foot**

$2 \text{ feet} - 1\dfrac{1}{8} \text{ feet}$

Start by drawing a line segment to represent 2 feet. We can break apart $1\dfrac{1}{8}$ into $1 + \dfrac{1}{8}$.

Starting with the whole numbers, we have 2 – 1 = 1, so we must cross off 1 whole foot.

We now must subtract $\dfrac{1}{8}$ from the remaining whole; partition the second foot into eighths,

and cross off one-eighth. We are left with $\dfrac{7}{8}$.

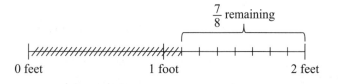

Thus, the difference between the longest and shortest distances is $\dfrac{7}{8}$ of a foot.

3. $3\frac{5}{8}$ **feet** The 3 shortest jumps are $1\frac{1}{8}$, $1\frac{1}{4}$, and $1\frac{1}{4}$. To find the total, we can use number lines.

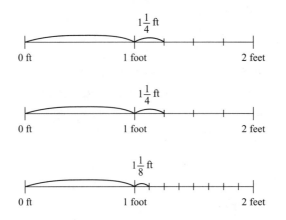

We have 3 whole feet (1 + 1 + 1) as well as three fractions of a foot ($\frac{1}{4} + \frac{1}{4} + \frac{1}{8}$).

To add the fractions, we must partition each fraction into eighths.

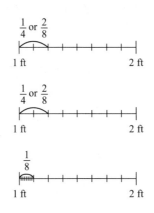

$\frac{2}{8} + \frac{2}{8} + \frac{1}{8} = \frac{5}{8}$

We now have 3 feet plus $\frac{5}{8}$ of a foot.

Thus, the sum of the 3 shortest jumps is $3\frac{5}{8}$ feet.

4. **(A)** Blaine, Davionna, and Savannah each jumped $1\frac{1}{4}$ feet. Their total can be shown with

addition: $1\frac{1}{4} + 1\frac{1}{4} + 1\frac{1}{4}$. This can also be shown as a multiplication problem: $3 \times 1\frac{1}{4}$.

Thus, the correct answer is **$3 \times 1\frac{1}{4}$**.

5. $1\frac{3}{8}$ **feet** To calculate how far each girl's jump would be if each jumped the same distance, we

would take the total distance, $5\frac{1}{2}$ feet, and share it evenly with the 4 girls.

In other words, divide $5\frac{1}{2}$ by 4. Because we are dealing with distance, a length model works well.

First, draw a line segment, and mark off $5\frac{1}{2}$ feet. Next, divide each foot into fourths. Also divide

the half-foot into fourths.

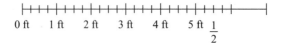

We now have 2 different lengths (the whole feet are divided into fourths, and the half foot is divided into much smaller pieces). To add, we need to make sure all lengths are the same. We can do this by dividing each foot into eighths.

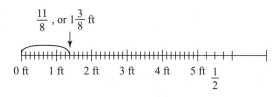

$\frac{11}{8}$, or $1\frac{3}{8}$ ft

0 ft   1 ft   2 ft   3 ft   4 ft   5 ft $\frac{1}{2}$

The $5\frac{1}{2}$ feet are now divided into 44 spaces. These spaces are being shared by 4 girls.

$44 \div 4 = 11$. So each girl will "jump" 11 of those spaces, or $1\frac{3}{8}$ feet.

6. **29 people; $14\frac{1}{2}$ minutes** By counting the *x*'s on the line plot, we can see that there were 29 swimmers who were timed. If every swimmer swam the length of the pool in half a minute, we can multiplying $29 \times \frac{1}{2}$. We can draw 29 halves on a number line. We can group 2 halves together to figure out how long a relay would last by make wholes. We now have 14 whole minutes plus half of a minute. Thus, the relay with 29 people would take $14\frac{1}{2}$ minutes.

7. **20 swimmers** A 5-minute relay shared among $\frac{1}{4}$-minute swimmers can be shown symbolically as $5 \div \frac{1}{4}$. We can work this problem out using a length model. Draw a number line and mark 5 sections to represent each of 5 minutes. Next, divide each minute into 4 equal sections.

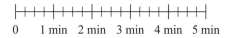

0   1 min   2 min   3 min   4 min   5 min

There are now 20 fourths. Since each swimmer will swim $\frac{1}{4}$ of a minute, and there are 20 fourths, this shows that 20 swimmers will be needed for the 5-minute relay.

8.

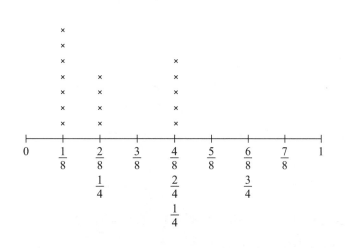

Understand and Measure Volume, page 116

1. **1 cubic unit**

2. Volume is the measure of the number of cubic units that fill a solid figure when filled without any gaps or overlaps.

3. **27 cubes**   There are 3 layers of cubes in Jimmy's puzzle, and each layer has 9 cubes. 3 layers of 9 means 3×9 which equals 27 cubes.

4. **12 cubic centimeters**   There are 2 layers of 6 cubic centimeters, which means there are 2×6 or 12 cubic centimeters.

5. **64 cubic inches**   There are 4 layers of 16 cubic inches. $4 \times 16 = 64$ cubic inches.

6. **20 cubic feet**   There are 2 layers of 10, which equals 20 cubic feet.

7. **54 cubic meters**   There are 6 layers of 9 cubic meters. $6 \times 9 = 54$ cubic meters.

8. **24 cubic units**   There are 3 layers of 8 cubic units. $3 \times 8 = 24$ cubic units.

Solve Volume Problems, page 118

1. Volume of cube A = 27 cubic units—3 layers of 9 cubes.

   Volume of cube B = 27 cubic units—same dimensions as cube A (3 by 3 by 3), which means they will have the same volume.

2. The volume of both of these rectangular prisms is the same. We can find the volume of the left rectangular prism by counting the number of cubes to fill it (2 layers of 10, or 20 cubes). The right figure has a length of 5, a width of 2, and a height of 2, which are the exact same dimensions of the rectangular prism on the left. Thus, both figures have the same volume.

3. A. Volume = length $\times$ width $\times$ height, OR width $\times$ height $\times$ length, OR height $\times$ width $\times$ length (order does not matter—the Commutative Property).

   B. Volume = base $\times$ height OR height $\times$ base.

4. **V = 192 cubic meters**   Length = 8 meters, width = 6 meters, height = 4 meters. To find the volume, multiply these 3 dimensions:

   Volume = length $\times$ width $\times$ height = $8 \times 6 \times 4 = 48 \times 4 = 192$ cubic meters.

5. **V = 96 cubic feet**   Volume = base $\times$ height = 12 square feet $\times$ 8 feet = 96 cubic feet.

6. **Possible answers: *w* = 1 and *l* = 12; *w* = 2 and *l* = 6; *w* = 3 and *l* = 4**

   Volume = length $\times$ width $\times$ height

   $72 = 6 \times w \times h$

   $72 = 6 \times \mathbf{12}$

   Possible factors of 12:

   1×12

   2×6

   3×4

   Thus, possible dimensions of this rectangular prism could be:

   $6 \times 1 \times 12$

   $6 \times 2 \times 6$

   $6 \times 3 \times 4$

7. **384 cubic inches**   The volume of this box is found by multiplying $12 \times 8 \times 4$, which equals 384 cubic inches.

8. **48 pieces**   To figure out how many $2 \times 2 \times 2$ inch candies can fit in the candy box, we must figure out the volume of 1 piece of candy: $2 \times 2 \times 2 = 8$ cubic inches. Dividing 384 by 8 will let us know how many pieces of candy fit into this box.

   $384 \div 8 = 48$ pieces of candy fit into the box

9. **V = 35 cubic units**   There are 2 cubes in this figure. The bottom cube has dimensions of 3 by 3 by 3. The top cube has dimensions of 2 by 2 by 2. Using the formula for volume, the bottom cube's volume is $3 \times 3 \times 3$, or 27 cubic units. The top cube's volume is $2 \times 2 \times 2$, or 8 cubic units. To find the total volume of both cubes, add $27 + 8 = 35$ cubic units.

10. **V = 28 cubic units**   One way to find the volume of this figure is to break it into 2 separate rectangular prisms. On the left, there is a figure with dimensions of 4 by 2 by 2, or $4 \times 2 \times 2 = 16$ cubic units. On the right, there is a figure with dimensions of 4 by 3 by 1, or $4 \times 3 \times 1 = 12$ cubic units. Adding them together, we have $16 + 12 = 28$ cubic units.

Understand the Coordinate Plane, page 122

1, 2, and 3.

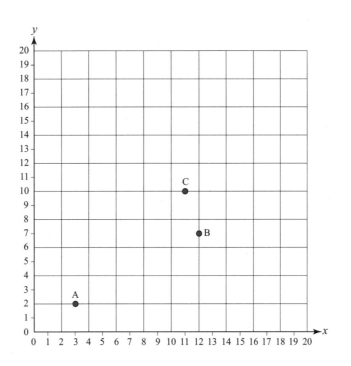

4. **(11, 10)**

5. To find a point on a coordinate graph for the ordered pair (6, 13), first find the origin. Then count 6 spaces away from zero to the right along the *x*-axis. From the point at 6 on the *x*-axis, count up 13 spaces along the *y*-axis. Draw a point where 6 on the *x*-axis and 13 on the *y*-axis intersect.

6.

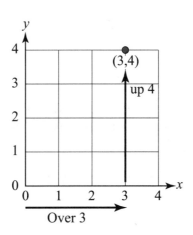

To graph (3, 4), first find 3 on the horizontal (*x*) axis, then follow the vertical (*y*) axis to 4.

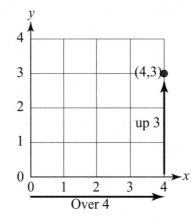

To graph (4, 3), first find 4 on the horizontal (*x*) axis, then follow the vertical (*y*) axis to 3.

7, 8, 9, and 10.

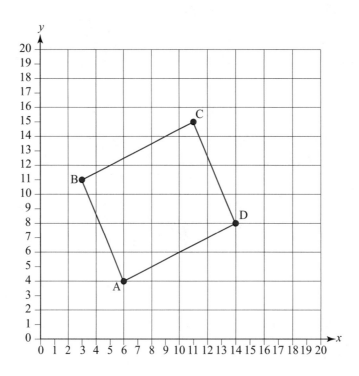

9. Answers will vary. The graph above is one possible solution.

    Point B: (3, 11)

    Point C: (11, 15)

10. Answers will vary based on the points chosen in question 9. Point D should form a parallelogram when connected, which means the opposite sides of the quadrilateral are parallel or equidistant from each other. For this example, Point D is the ordered pair (14, 8).

1.

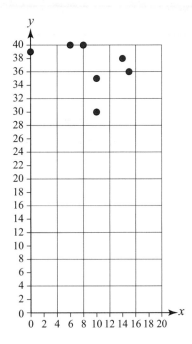

2. **Point A**

3. (9, 45)

4. First find the point that is 9 spaces from 0 on the *x*-axis. Next, move up along the *y*-axis to 40. Draw the point where 9 on the *x*-axis and 40 on the *y*-axis intersect.

5. A. Answers will vary. The point (3, 9) must be graphed, as well as 4 other points directly beside that point. Here is a possible solution:

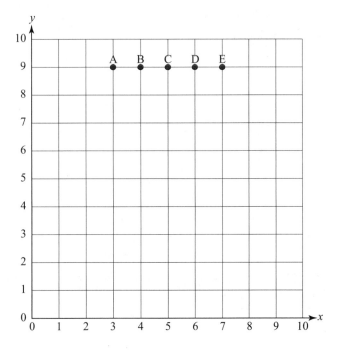

B. A (3, 9), B (4, 9), C (5, 9), D (6, 9), E (7, 9)

6.

Number of Minutes	Number of Laps	Ordered Pair
1	3	(1, 3)
2	6	(2, 6)
3	9	(3, 9)
4	12	(4, 12)
5	15	(5, 15)
6	18	(6, 18)

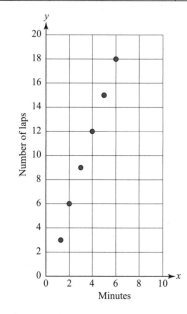

7. Each minute, Lisa swims 3 laps (1 × 3). If she swims for 10 minutes, she will swim 30 laps (10 × 3). If she swims 20 minutes, she will swim 60 laps (20 × 3).

For each ordered pair, the *y*-value is 3 times the *x*-value.

8. Answers will vary. A possible solution is graphed below:

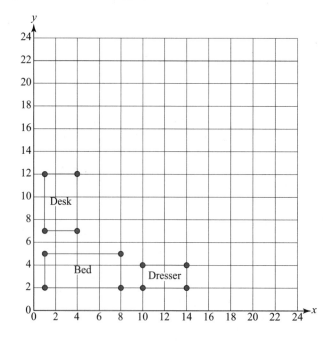

9. Bed: (1, 2), (1, 5), (8, 5), (8, 2)

   Desk: (1, 7), (1, 12), (4, 12), (4, 7)

   Dresser: (10, 2), (10, 4), (14, 4), (14, 2)

10. If the bed is shifted 3 feet along the *x*-axis, we simply add 3 to the *x*-coordinate. For the above example, ordered pairs for the bed would become:

    Bed: (4, 2), (4, 5), (11, 5), (11, 2)

Understand Attributes of Two-Dimensional Figures, page 132

1.

Shape	⬠	⬠	▱	◇	▭	◻
Quadrilateral	X	X	X	X	X	X
Trapezoid		X				
Parallelogram			X	X	X	X
Rhombus				X		X
Rectangle					X	X
Square						X

2. **True** A rectangle is a quadrilateral with 4 right angles. Because a square has 4 right angles, by definition it is also considered a rectangle.

3. **True** A rhombus is a quadrilateral with 4 congruent sides. A square is a special type of rhombus; in addition to 4 congruent sides, a square also has 4 right angles.

4. **False** Parallelograms must have 2 pairs of parallel sides. To also be a rectangle, a parallelogram must have 4 right angles. Not all parallelograms have 4 right angles.

5. **True** All trapezoids have 4 sides, which make them all quadrilaterals.

6. This shape is called a trapezoid.

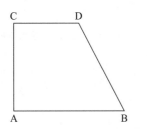

7. This shape is called a rhombus.

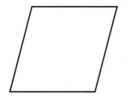

8. This shape is called a rectangle.

9. A parallelogram cannot also be a trapezoid because by definition, a parallelogram has 2 pairs of parallel sides, but a trapezoid by definition only has 1 pair of parallel sides.

10. The description must have the following important facts included:
    - quadrilateral (4 sides)
    - 4 congruent sides
    - parallelogram (2 pairs of parallel sides)

Classify Two-Dimensional Figures, page 136

1. Figure Q is an equilateral triangle because all 3 sides are of equal length.

2. Figure S is an isosceles triangle because 2 sides are of equal length.

3. Figures R and T are scalene triangles because all 3 sides are different lengths.

4. Figure R is a right triangle because it has 1 right (90 degree) angle.

5. Both Figure Q and Figure S are acute triangles because all 3 angles are acute (less than 90 degrees) angles.

6. Figure T is an obtuse triangle because it has 1 obtuse (greater than 90 degrees) angle.

7. right and scalene

8. obtuse and isosceles

9. quadrilateral, parallelogram, rectangle

10. quadrilateral, parallelogram, rhombus

Math Practice Test, page 140

1. **(D)** We must do what is in parentheses first. In parentheses, we have $10 - 4 \times 2$. Next, we multiply before subtracting. Therefore, 4×2 should be done first. (5.OA.A.1)

2. **35** $55 \div (4 + 7) \times 6 + (15 \div 3)$

   Parentheses first: $55 \div 11 \times 6 + 5$

   Multiply or divide in the order they appear: $5 \times 6 + 5$

   $30 + 5 = 35$ (5.OA.A.1)

3. **(C)** Operations in parentheses must be done first, which means $(6 + 9)$ and $(12 \div 4)$ are completed before they are multiplied. Subtracting 3 is the last step. (5.OA.A.2)

4. $(7 \times 12) + (110 \div 5)$

Parentheses indicate that the product and quotient must be done first, then added. (5.OA.A.3)

5. **(A)**

$0 \times 4 = 0$

$2 \times 4 = 8$

$3 \times 4 = 12$

$4 \times 4 = 16$ (5.OA.A.3)

6. **(B)** Because $7.4 \times 10 = 74$, we know that $\frac{1}{10}$ of 74 is 7.4. (5.NBT.A.1)

7. **4.8** Patterns with zeros and decimals show that 10 times any number shifts the decimal point 1 place to the right, from in front of the 4 (0.48) to in front of the 8 (4.8). (5.NBT.A.1)

8. *

1. **F** $58 \times \frac{1}{1,000} = 0.058$

2. **E** $58 \times 100 = 5,800$

3. **B** $58 \times \frac{1}{100} = 0.58$

4. **A** $58 \times 1 = 58$

5. **D** $58 \times \frac{1}{10} = 5.8$

6. **C** $58 \times 10 = 580$

7. **G** $58 \times 1,000 = 58,000$ (5.NBT.A.2)

*Multiplying by 10, 100, or 1,000 moves the decimal point 1, 2, or 3 places to the **right**.

*Multiplying by $\frac{1}{10}$, $\frac{1}{100}$, or $\frac{1}{1,000}$ moves the decimal point 1, 2, or 3 places to the **left**.

9. **(C)** In the problem $0.29 \times \underline{\hspace{1cm}} = 290$, the decimal moves 3 places to the right, so 3 zeros are needed in the factor. (5.NBT.A.2)

10. $47.295 = 4 \times 10 + 7 \times 1 + 2 \times 1/10 + 9 \times \frac{1}{100} + 5 \times \frac{1}{1,000}$ (5.NBT.A.3)

11. Three hundred forty-six and seven hundred twenty-nine thousandths (5.NBT.A.3)

12. **(D)** To compare these numbers, we can add a zero to 43.83 so that both numbers are in the thousandths.

43.827   43.83**0**

Because 827 < 830, we know that 43.827 < 43.83**0**. (5.NBT.A.3)

13. **(C)** Looking at the place value of 5.47, we have 4 tenths and 7 hundredths. We can underline the 4, and look at the place to the right.

5.<u>4</u>7   7 is greater than 5, which means we would round the tenths to the next number, 5. Thus, 5.47 to the nearest tenth is 5.5. (5.NBT.A.4)

14. **Both 8.536 and 8.538.**   Both have a 3 in the hundredths but have digits higher than 5 in the thousandths place, which means both decimals round up to 8.54. (5.NBT.A.4)

15. **26,752**

$$\begin{array}{r} {}^{33}3{}^{1\,1}52 \\ \times \quad 76 \\ \hline 2112 \\ +\ 24640 \\ \hline 26,752 \end{array}$$ (5.NBT.A.5)

16. **(D)**

$$
\begin{array}{r}
{}^{1}1{}^{1}3 2 5 \\
\times\ \ \ \ 27 \\
\hline
8\ 7\ 5 \\
+\ 2500 \\
\hline
3,375
\end{array}
$$
(5.NBT.A.5)

17. **232**   200 + 30 + 2 = 232 (5.NBT.A.6)

$$
\begin{array}{r}
6\overline{)1,392} \\
-\ 1,200\ \ (200\times6) \\
\hline
192 \\
-\ 180\ \ (30\times6) \\
\hline
12 \\
-\ 12\ \ (2\times6) \\
\hline
0 \\
\end{array}
$$

200 + 30 + 2 = 232

200	30	2
200	30	2
200	30	2
200	30	2
200	30	2
200	30	2

18. **23 jelly beans per classmate, with 21 left over.**

Think Space

23 × 1 = 23
23 × 2 = 46
23 × 10 = 230
23 × 20 = 460

Area Model

$$
\begin{array}{r}
4\ 1 \\
23\overline{)550} \\
-\ 460 \\
\hline
{}^{8}\!\!\not9 10 \\
-\ 46 \\
\hline
44 \\
-\ 23 \\
\hline
21
\end{array}
$$

Think Space

23 × 2 = 46
23 × 10 = 230
23 × 20 = 460

Area Model

	20	+	2	+	1
23	460		46		23

20 + 2 + 1 = 23 jelly beans per classmate, with 21 left over. (5.NBT.A.7)

19. **(C)**

$$
\begin{array}{r}
\$\ {}^{5}3{}^{3}9.50 \\
\times\ \ \ \ \ \ 16 \\
\hline
{}^{1}2{}^{1}3700 \\
39500 \\
\hline
\$\ 632.00
\end{array}
$$

20. **$177.55**   To find how much money Angelo has left, we must subtract $72.45 from $250. To do this, we must first rewrite $250 as $250.00 to compute with $72.45. Lining up the decimals, we can then subtract.

$$
\begin{array}{r}
\$\ {}^{1}2{}^{14}5{}^{9}0.{}^{9}0{}^{1}0 \\
-\ \ \ \ 72.45 \\
\hline
\$\ 177.55
\end{array}
$$

Angelo has $177.55 left. (5.NBT.A.7)

21.

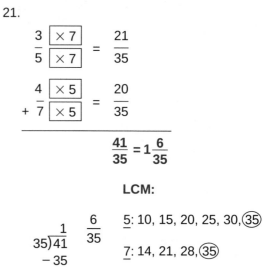

$$
\dfrac{3}{5}\ \boxed{\times 7\atop \times 7} = \dfrac{21}{35}
$$

$$
+\ \dfrac{4}{7}\ \boxed{\times 5\atop \times 5} = \dfrac{20}{35}
$$

$$
\dfrac{41}{35} = 1\dfrac{6}{35}
$$

LCM:

$$
\begin{array}{r}
\ \ \ 1 \\
35\overline{)41} \\
-\ 35 \\
\hline
6
\end{array}
\qquad \dfrac{6}{35}
$$

5: 10, 15, 20, 25, 30, ㉟

7: 14, 21, 28, ㉟

22. **(B)**

$$
5\dfrac{1}{2}\ \boxed{\times 3\atop \times 3} = 5\dfrac{3}{6}
$$

$$
-2\dfrac{1}{3}\ \boxed{\times 2\atop \times 2} = -2\dfrac{2}{6}
$$

$$
= 3\dfrac{1}{6}
$$

LCM:

2: 2, 4, ⑥, 8

3: 3, ⑥, 9

23. $\frac{11}{30}$ **of a candy bar; less than**

$$\frac{1}{6} + \frac{1}{5} = \frac{5}{30} + \frac{6}{30} = \frac{11}{30}$$

The boys ate $\frac{11}{30}$ of the candy bar, which is less than half of the candy bar ($\frac{15}{30}$ is $\frac{1}{2}$).

Thus, there is more than $\frac{1}{2}$ of the candy bar left. (5.NF.A.2)

24. **$6\frac{1}{6}$ yards** Draw 10 squares to represent 10 yards of fabric.

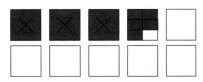

Her pattern uses 3 whole yards, so mark out 3 squares. She also uses $\frac{5}{6}$ of a square, so divide another square into 6 pieces, and shade 5 of them.

The remaining fabric (which isn't crossed out) is equal to 6 whole yards and $\frac{1}{6}$ of a yard, or $6\frac{1}{6}$ yards. (5.NF.A.2)

25. **C and E** Selected situations are those that can be interpreted or simplified to 3 divided by 5 or 3 out of 5. (5.NF.B.3)

26. **(B)** This situation can be reworded as "40 boxes divided among 3 families," or $\frac{40}{3}$, which simplifies to $13\frac{1}{3}$ boxes. (5.NF.B.3)

27. For this problem, we can think "$\frac{1}{3}$ of $\frac{2}{5}$". Draw a rectangle, and shade in $\frac{2}{5}$ of it.

Then partition the whole into thirds, and shade in $\frac{1}{3}$ of it.

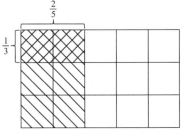

We now have 15 pieces, and 2 of the 15 pieces are shaded by both the fifths and the thirds. Thus, $\frac{1}{3} \times \frac{2}{5} = \frac{2}{15}$. (5.NF.B.4)

28. $\frac{12}{20}$ **of a yard** Draw a rectangle to represent the garden, partition it vertically into fifths and shade in 4 of them. Then partition it horizontally into fourths, and shade in 3 of them.

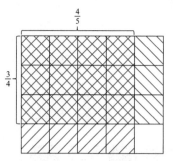

We now have 20 sections, and 12 of them are shaded by both the fifths and the fourths. Thus, $\frac{12}{20}$ of a yard is the area of the Smiths' garden. (5.NF.B.4)

29. **(D)**

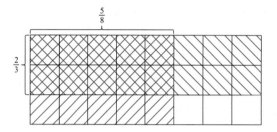

(5.NF.B.4)

30. **(B)** "$\frac{5}{8} \times \frac{1}{2}$" means that we are taking a fraction of $\frac{1}{2}$, which is a piece of $\frac{1}{2}$.

Thus, the product will be smaller than both factors. (5.NF.B.5)

31. $2 \times \frac{3}{8}$ **is larger.** With $\frac{2}{5} \times \frac{3}{8}$, we are taking a fraction of a fraction, which is a small piece.

With $2 \times \frac{3}{8}$, we have 2 sets of $\frac{3}{8}$, which is more than $\frac{2}{5}$ of a set of $\frac{3}{8}$ (5.NF.B.5)

32. **$45.50** $7 for $6\frac{1}{2}$ hours means 7×6 plus $7 \times \frac{1}{2}$.

$7 \times 6 = 42$

$7 \times \frac{1}{2} = 3\frac{1}{2}$

$42 + 3\frac{1}{2} = 45\frac{1}{2}$, or $45.50. Thus, Sadie will make $45.50 if she babysits for $6\frac{1}{2}$ hours. (5.NF.B.6)

33. $\frac{3}{8}$ **of a pie** Draw a circle to represent a pie, and cut it into fourths. Shade in 1 of the fourths to show what has already been eaten.

Then divide each of the remaining fourths into 2 parts, and shade 1 out of every 2 parts to show what portion Emily ate.

There are 3 pieces left, and each piece is $\frac{1}{8}$. Thus, $\frac{3}{8}$ of the pie is left. (5.NF.B.6)

34. Answer will vary. The story should involve having 4 whole objects, and they are being divided into fifths, so that the answer is 20.

A possible story might be: There are 4 pizzas that are cut into fifths. How many pieces will there be? (5.NF.B.7)

35. **$\frac{2}{15}$ of the bottle** This situation is $\frac{2}{3} \div 5$. Draw a rectangle to represent a bottle, and shade in $\frac{2}{3}$. Then partition the $\frac{2}{3}$ into 5 pieces.

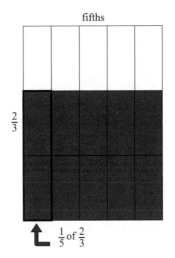

fifths

$\frac{2}{3}$

$\frac{1}{5}$ of $\frac{2}{3}$

We now have 15 parts of the bottle. If each friend gets $\frac{1}{5}$ of the $\frac{2}{3}$, that means each gets 2 pieces of the 15, or $\frac{2}{15}$ of the bottle of soda. (5.NF.B.7)

36. **(A)** Breanna—62 inches

Myquisha—5 feet 4 inches = 5 × 12 + 4 = 60 + 4 = 64 inches

Ariana – 1 yard, 2 feet, 7 inches = 36 inches + 24 inches + 7 inches = 67 inches

Thus, in order from shortest to longest, the correct answer is (A). (5.MD.A.1)

37. **26 cups** Because 1 cup is 8 ounces, we can create a conversion chart for cups using what we know about parts of a gallon.

1 cup = 8 ounces
1 pint = 2 cups
1 quart = 2 pints = 4 cups
1 gallon = 4 quarts = 8 pints = 16 cups

The recipe has 1 gallon of water, or 16 cups.
It has 2 quarts of seltzer, or 4 cups plus 4 cups or 8 cups.

It has 1 pint of lime juice, or 2 cups.

Total amount of liquid is 16 + 8 + 2 cups, or 26 cups of limeade. (5.MD.A.1)

38.

			x								
		x	x								
	x	x	x		x	x	x				

10 yrs.	$\frac{1}{12}$	$\frac{2}{12}$	$\frac{3}{12}$	$\frac{4}{12}$	$\frac{5}{12}$	$\frac{6}{12}$	$\frac{7}{12}$	$\frac{8}{12}$	$\frac{9}{12}$	$\frac{10}{12}$	$\frac{11}{12}$	11 yrs.
	$\frac{1}{6}$	$\frac{1}{4}$	$\frac{1}{3}$		$\frac{1}{2}$			$\frac{2}{3}$	$\frac{3}{4}$	$\frac{5}{6}$		

39. **$\frac{1}{2}$ a year** $10\frac{7}{12} - 10\frac{1}{12} = \frac{6}{12}$ or $\frac{1}{2}$

The difference between the youngest and oldest in this group is $\frac{1}{2}$ of a year. (5.MD.A.2)

40. Volume is the measure of how many units fill a solid figure. We can find the volume of a solid figure if we know the length, width, and height of the figure. The formula to find the volume of a cube or rectangular prism is length × width × height.

    $V = l \times w \times h$ (5.MD.C.3)

41. **12 cubic units**   There are 2 layers of 6 cubes. We can also multiply $2 \times 2 \times 3 = 12$ cubic units. (5.MD.C.3)

42. **64 cubic units**   There are 4 layers of 16 cubes: $4 \times 16 = 64$ cubic units, or $4 \times 4 \times 4 = 64$ cubic units. (5.MD.C.4)

43. **(D)**   448 cubic cm—$7 \times 8 \times 8 = 448$ cubic cm. (5.MD.C.5)

44. **$3 \times 5 \times 3 = 45$ cubic feet.** (5.MD.C.5)

45. **There are 11 cubes on the side facing us.** There are 4 "layers" of 11. $4 \times 11 = 44$ cubes. (5.MD.C.5)

46.

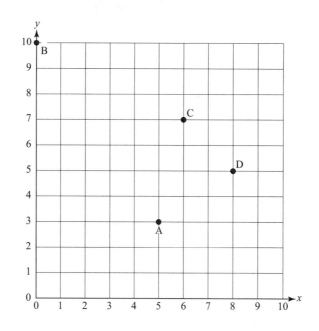

(5.G.A.1)

47. **Rectangle, Rhombus, Parallelogram, Quadrilateral**

    A square is a rectangle because it has 4 right angles.

    A square is a rhombus because all 4 sides are equivalent.

    A square is a parallelogram because it has 2 pairs of parallel sides.

    A square is a quadrilateral because it has 4 sides.

    A square is NOT a trapezoid because a trapezoid has only 1 pair of parallel sides. (5.G.A.3)

48.

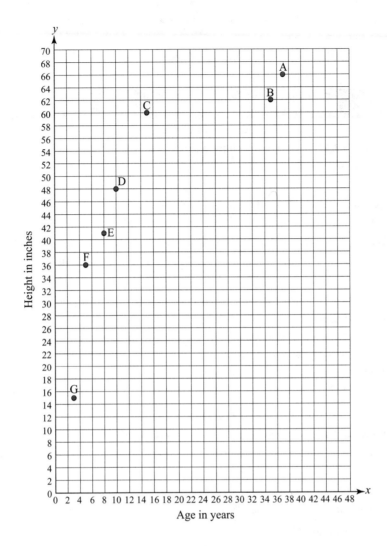

(5.G.A.2)

49. **(B)** (5.G.B.3)

50. **(D)** This triangle has 1 obtuse angle (greater than 90 degrees) and 2 equivalent sides. (5.G.B.4)

APPENDIX A

ENGLISH LANGUAGE ARTS STANDARDS

Reading: Literature

Key Ideas and Details

CCSS.ELA-LITERACY.RL.5.1 Quote accurately from a text when explaining what the text says explicitly and when drawing inferences from the text.

CCSS.ELA-LITERACY.RL.5.2 Determine a theme of a story, drama, or poem from details in the text, including how characters in a story or drama respond to challenges or how the speaker in a poem reflects upon a topic; summarize the text.

CCSS.ELA-LITERACY.RL.5.3 Compare and contrast two or more characters, settings, or events in a story or drama, drawing on specific details in the text (e.g., how characters interact).

Craft and Structure

CCSS.ELA-LITERACY.RL.5.4 Determine the meaning of words and phrases as they are used in a text, including figurative language such as metaphors and similes.

CCSS.ELA-LITERACY.RL.5.5 Explain how a series of chapters, scenes, or stanzas fits together to provide the overall structure of a particular story, drama, or poem.

CCSS.ELA-LITERACY.RL.5.6 Describe how a narrator's or speaker's point of view influences how events are described.

Integration of Knowledge and Ideas

CCSS.ELA-LITERACY.RL.5.7 Analyze how visual and multimedia elements contribute to the meaning, tone, or beauty of a text (e.g., graphic novel, multimedia presentation of fiction, folktale, myth, poem).

CCSS.ELA-LITERACY.RL.5.8 (RL.5.8 not applicable to literature)

CCSS.ELA-LITERACY.RL.5.9 Compare and contrast stories in the same genre (e.g., mysteries and adventure stories) on their approaches to similar themes and topics.

Range of Reading and Level of Text Complexity

CCSS.ELA-LITERACY.RL.5.10 By the end of the year, read and comprehend literature, including stories, dramas, and poetry, at the high end of the grades 4–5 text complexity band independently and proficiently.

Reading: Informational Text

Key Ideas and Details

CCSS.ELA-LITERACY.RI.5.1 Quote accurately from a text when explaining what the text says explicitly and when drawing inferences from the text.

CCSS.ELA-LITERACY.RI.5.2 Determine two or more main ideas of a text and explain how they are supported by key details; summarize the text.

CCSS.ELA-LITERACY.RI.5.3 Explain the relationships or interactions between two or more individuals, events, ideas, or concepts in a historical, scientific, or technical text based on specific information in the text.

Craft and Structure

CCSS.ELA-LITERACY.RI.5.4 Determine the meaning of general academic and domain-specific words and phrases in a text relevant to a *grade 5 topic or subject area*.

CCSS.ELA-LITERACY.RI.5.5 Compare and contrast the overall structure (e.g., chronology, comparison, cause/effect, problem/solution) of events, ideas, concepts, or information in two or more texts.

CCSS.ELA-LITERACY.RI.5.6 Analyze multiple accounts of the same event or topic, noting important similarities and differences in the point of view they represent.

Integration of Knowledge and Ideas

CCSS.ELA-LITERACY.RI.5.7 Draw on information from multiple print or digital sources, demonstrating the ability to locate an answer to a question quickly or to solve a problem efficiently.

CCSS.ELA-LITERACY.RI.5.8 Explain how an author uses reasons and evidence to support particular points in a text, identifying which reasons and evidence support which point(s).

CCSS.ELA-LITERACY.RI.5.9 Integrate information from several texts on the same topic in order to write or speak about the subject knowledgeably.

Range of Reading and Level of Text Complexity

CCSS.ELA-LITERACY.RI.5.10 By the end of the year, read and comprehend informational texts, including history/social studies, science, and technical texts, at the high end of the grades 4–5 text complexity band independently and proficiently.

Reading: Foundational Skills

Phonics and Word Recognition

CCSS.ELA-LITERACY.RF.5.3 Know and apply grade-level phonics and word analysis skills in decoding words.

CCSS.ELA-LITERACY.RF.5.3.A

Use combined knowledge of all letter-sound correspondences, syllabication patterns, and morphology (e.g., roots and affixes) to read accurately unfamiliar multisyllabic words in context and out of context.

Fluency

CCSS.ELA-LITERACY.RF.5.4 Read with sufficient accuracy and fluency to support comprehension.

CCSS.ELA-LITERACY.RF.5.4.A

Read grade-level text with purpose and understanding.

CCSS.ELA-LITERACY.RF.5.4.B

Read grade-level prose and poetry orally with accuracy, appropriate rate, and expression on successive readings.

CCSS.ELA-LITERACY.RF.5.4.C

Use context to confirm or self-correct word recognition and understanding, rereading as necessary.

Writing

Text Types and Purposes

CCSS.ELA-LITERACY.W.5.1 Write opinion pieces on topics or texts, supporting a point of view with reasons and information.

CCSS.ELA-LITERACY.W.5.1.A

Introduce a topic or text clearly, state an opinion, and create an organizational structure in which ideas are logically grouped to support the writer's purpose.

CCSS.ELA-LITERACY.W.5.1.B

Provide logically ordered reasons that are supported by facts and details.

CCSS.ELA-LITERACY.W.5.1.C

Link opinion and reasons using words, phrases, and clauses (e.g., *consequently*, *specifically*).

CCSS.ELA-LITERACY.W.5.1.D

Provide a concluding statement or section related to the opinion presented.

CCSS.ELA-LITERACY.W.5.2 Write informative/explanatory texts to examine a topic and convey ideas and information clearly.

CCSS.ELA-LITERACY.W.5.2.A

Introduce a topic clearly, provide a general observation and focus, and group related information logically; include formatting (e.g., headings), illustrations, and multimedia when useful to aiding comprehension.

CCSS.ELA-LITERACY.W.5.2.B

Develop the topic with facts, definitions, concrete details, quotations, or other information and examples related to the topic.

CCSS.ELA-LITERACY.W.5.2.C

Link ideas within and across categories of information using words, phrases, and clauses (e.g., *in contrast*, *especially*).

CCSS.ELA-LITERACY.W.5.2.D

Use precise language and domain-specific vocabulary to inform about or explain the topic.

CCSS.ELA-LITERACY.W.5.2.E

Provide a concluding statement or section related to the information or explanation presented.

CCSS.ELA-LITERACY.W.5.3 Write narratives to develop real or imagined experiences or events using effective technique, descriptive details, and clear event sequences.

CCSS.ELA-LITERACY.W.5.3.A

Orient the reader by establishing a situation and introducing a narrator and/or characters; organize an event sequence that unfolds naturally.

CCSS.ELA-LITERACY.W.5.3.B

Use narrative techniques, such as dialogue, description, and pacing, to develop experiences and events or show the responses of characters to situations.

CCSS.ELA-LITERACY.W.5.3.C

Use a variety of transitional words, phrases, and clauses to manage the sequence of events.

CCSS.ELA-LITERACY.W.5.3.D

Use concrete words and phrases and sensory details to convey experiences and events precisely.

CCSS.ELA-LITERACY.W.5.3.E

Provide a conclusion that follows from the narrated experiences or events.

Production and Distribution of Writing

CCSS.ELA-LITERACY.W.5.4 Produce clear and coherent writing in which the development and organization are appropriate to task, purpose, and audience. (Grade-specific expectations for writing types are defined in standards 1–3 above.)

CCSS.ELA-LITERACY.W.5.5 With guidance and support from peers and adults, develop and strengthen writing as needed by planning, revising, editing, rewriting, or trying a new approach. (Editing for conventions should demonstrate command of Language standards 1–3, up to and including grade 5 here.)

CCSS.ELA-LITERACY.W.5.6 With some guidance and support from adults, use technology, including the Internet, to produce and publish writing as well as to interact and collaborate with others; demonstrate sufficient command of keyboarding skills to type a minimum of two pages in a single sitting.

Research to Build and Present Knowledge

CCSS.ELA-LITERACY.W.5.7 Conduct short research projects that use several sources to build knowledge through investigation of different aspects of a topic.

CCSS.ELA-LITERACY.W.5.8 Recall relevant information from experiences or gather relevant information from print and digital sources; summarize or paraphrase information in notes and finished work, and provide a list of sources.

CCSS.ELA-LITERACY.W.5.9 Draw evidence from literary or informational texts to support analysis, reflection, and research.

CCSS.ELA-LITERACY.W.5.9.A

Apply *grade 5 Reading standards* to literature (e.g., "Compare and contrast two or more characters, settings, or events in a story or a drama, drawing on specific details in the text [e.g., how characters interact]").

CCSS.ELA-LITERACY.W.5.9.B

Apply *grade 5 Reading standards* to informational texts (e.g., "Explain how an author uses reasons and evidence to support particular points in a text, identifying which reasons and evidence support which point[s]").

Range of Writing

CCSS.ELA-LITERACY.W.5.10 Write routinely over extended time frames (time for research, reflection, and revision) and shorter time frames (a single sitting or a day or two) for a range of discipline-specific tasks, purposes, and audiences.

Speaking & Listening

Comprehension and Collaboration

CCSS.ELA-LITERACY.SL.5.1 Engage effectively in a range of collaborative discussions (one-on-one, in groups, and teacher-led) with diverse partners on *grade 5 topics and texts*, building on others' ideas and expressing their own clearly.

CCSS.ELA-LITERACY.SL.5.1.A

Come to discussions prepared, having read or studied required material; explicitly draw on that preparation and other information known about the topic to explore ideas under discussion.

CCSS.ELA-LITERACY.SL.5.1.B

Follow agreed-upon rules for discussions and carry out assigned roles.

CCSS.ELA-LITERACY.SL.5.1.C

Pose and respond to specific questions by making comments that contribute to the discussion and elaborate on the remarks of others.

CCSS.ELA-LITERACY.SL.5.1.D

Review the key ideas expressed and draw conclusions in light of information and knowledge gained from the discussions.

CCSS.ELA-LITERACY.SL.5.2 Summarize a written text read aloud or information presented in diverse media and formats, including visually, quantitatively, and orally.

CCSS.ELA-LITERACY.SL.5.3 Summarize the points a speaker makes and explain how each claim is supported by reasons and evidence.

Presentation of Knowledge and Ideas

CCSS.ELA-LITERACY.SL.5.4 Report on a topic or text or present an opinion, sequencing ideas logically and using appropriate facts and relevant, descriptive details to support main ideas or themes; speak clearly at an understandable pace.

CCSS.ELA-LITERACY.SL.5.5 Include multimedia components (e.g., graphics, sound) and visual displays in presentations when appropriate to enhance the development of main ideas or themes.

CCSS.ELA-LITERACY.SL.5.6 Adapt speech to a variety of contexts and tasks, using formal English when appropriate to task and situation. (See grade 5 Language standards 1 and 3 here for specific expectations.)

Language

Conventions of Standard English

CCSS.ELA-LITERACY.L.5.1 Demonstrate command of the conventions of standard English grammar and usage when writing or speaking.

CCSS.ELA-LITERACY.L.5.1.A

Explain the function of conjunctions, prepositions, and interjections in general and their function in particular sentences.

CCSS.ELA-LITERACY.L.5.1.B

Form and use the perfect (e.g., *I had walked; I have walked; I will have walked*) verb tenses.

CCSS.ELA-LITERACY.L.5.1.C

Use verb tense to convey various times, sequences, states, and conditions.

CCSS.ELA-LITERACY.L.5.1.D

Recognize and correct inappropriate shifts in verb tense.

CCSS.ELA-LITERACY.L.5.1.E

Use correlative conjunctions (e.g., *either/or, neither/nor*).

CCSS.ELA-LITERACY.L.5.2 Demonstrate command of the conventions of standard English capitalization, punctuation, and spelling when writing.

CCSS.ELA-LITERACY.L.5.2.A

Use punctuation to separate items in a series.

CCSS.ELA-LITERACY.L.5.2.B

Use a comma to separate an introductory element from the rest of the sentence.

CCSS.ELA-LITERACY.L.5.2.C

Use a comma to set off the words *yes* and *no* (e.g., *Yes, thank you*), to set off a tag question from the rest of the sentence (e.g., *It's true, isn't it?*), and to indicate direct address (e.g., *Is that you, Steve?*).

CCSS.ELA-LITERACY.L.5.2.D

Use underlining, quotation marks, or italics to indicate titles of works.

CCSS.ELA-LITERACY.L.5.2.E

Spell grade-appropriate words correctly, consulting references as needed.

Knowledge of Language

CCSS.ELA-LITERACY.L.5.3 Use knowledge of language and its conventions when writing, speaking, reading, or listening.

CCSS.ELA-LITERACY.L.5.3.A

Expand, combine, and reduce sentences for meaning, reader/listener interest, and style.

CCSS.ELA-LITERACY.L.5.3.B

Compare and contrast the varieties of English (e.g., *dialects, registers*) used in stories, dramas, or poems.

Vocabulary Acquisition and Use

CCSS.ELA-LITERACY.L.5.4 Determine or clarify the meaning of unknown and multiple-meaning words and phrases based on grade 5 reading and content, choosing flexibly from a range of strategies.

CCSS.ELA-LITERACY.L.5.4.A

Use context (e.g., cause/effect relationships and comparisons in text) as a clue to the meaning of a word or phrase.

CCSS.ELA-LITERACY.L.5.4.B

Use common, grade-appropriate Greek and Latin affixes and roots as clues to the meaning of a word (e.g., *photograph, photosynthesis*).

CCSS.ELA-LITERACY.L.5.4.C

Consult reference materials (e.g., dictionaries, glossaries, thesauruses), both print and digital, to find the pronunciation and determine or clarify the precise meaning of key words and phrases.

CCSS.ELA-LITERACY.L.5.5 Demonstrate understanding of figurative language, word relationships, and nuances in word meanings.

CCSS.ELA-LITERACY.L.5.5.A

Interpret figurative language, including similes and metaphors, in context.

CCSS.ELA-LITERACY.L.5.5.B

Recognize and explain the meaning of common idioms, adages, and proverbs.

CCSS.ELA-LITERACY.L.5.5.C

Use the relationship between particular words (e.g., synonyms, antonyms, homographs) to better understand each of the words.

CCSS.ELA-LITERACY.L.5.6 Acquire and use accurately grade-appropriate general academic and domain-specific words and phrases, including those that signal contrast, addition, and other logical relationships (e.g., *however, although, nevertheless, similarly, moreover, in addition*).

APPENDIX B
MATHEMATICS STANDARDS

Operations and Algebraic Thinking

Write and interpret numerical expressions

CCSS.MATH.CONTENT.5.OA.A.1 Use parentheses, brackets, or braces in numerical expressions, and evaluate expressions with these symbols.

CCSS.MATH.CONTENT.5.OA.A.2 Write simple expressions that record calculations with numbers, and interpret numerical expressions without evaluating them. *For example, express the calculation "add 8 and 7, then multiply by 2" as $2 \times (8 + 7)$. Recognize that $3 \times (18932 + 921)$ is three times as large as $18932 + 921$, without having to calculate the indicated sum or product.*

Analyze patterns and relationships

CCSS.MATH.CONTENT.5.OA.B.3 Generate two numerical patterns using two given rules. Identify apparent relationships between corresponding terms. Form ordered pairs consisting of corresponding terms from the two patterns, and graph the ordered pairs on a coordinate plane. *For example, given the rule "Add 3" and the starting number 0, and given the rule "Add 6" and the starting number 0, generate terms in the resulting sequences, and observe that the terms in one sequence are twice the corresponding terms in the other sequence. Explain informally why this is so.*

Number and Operations in Base Ten

Understand the place value system

CCSS.MATH.CONTENT.5.NBT.A.1 Recognize that in a multi-digit number, a digit in one place represents 10 times as much as it represents in the place to its right and 1/10 of what it represents in the place to its left.

CCSS.MATH.CONTENT.5.NBT.A.2 Explain patterns in the number of zeros of the product when multiplying a number by powers of 10, and explain patterns in the placement of the decimal point when a decimal is multiplied or divided by a power of 10. Use whole-number exponents to denote powers of 10.

CCSS.MATH.CONTENT.5.NBT.A.3 Read, write, and compare decimals to thousandths.

> **CCSS.MATH.CONTENT.5.NBT.A.3.A**
>
> Read and write decimals to thousandths using base-ten numerals, number names, and expanded form, e.g., $347.392 = 3 \times 100 + 4 \times 10 + 7 \times 1 + 3 \times (1/10) + 9 \times (1/100) + 2 \times (1/1000)$.
>
> **CCSS.MATH.CONTENT.5.NBT.A.3.B**
>
> Compare two decimals to thousandths based on meanings of the digits in each place, using >, =, and < symbols to record the results of comparisons.

CCSS.MATH.CONTENT.5.NBT.A.4 Use place value understanding to round decimals to any place.

Perform operations with multi-digit whole numbers and with decimals to hundredths

CCSS.MATH.CONTENT.5.NBT.B.5 Fluently multiply multi-digit whole numbers using the standard algorithm.

CCSS.MATH.CONTENT.5.NBT.B.6 Find whole-number quotients of whole numbers with up to four-digit dividends and two-digit divisors, using strategies based on place value, the properties of operations, and/or the relationship between multiplication and division. Illustrate and explain the calculation by using equations, rectangular arrays, and/or area models.

CCSS.MATH.CONTENT.5.NBT.B.7 Add, subtract, multiply, and divide decimals to hundredths, using concrete models or drawings and strategies based on place value, properties of operations, and/or the relationship between addition and subtraction; relate the strategy to a written method and explain the reasoning used.

Use equivalent fractions as a strategy to add and subtract fractions

CCSS.MATH.CONTENT.5.NF.A.1 Add and subtract fractions with unlike denominators (including mixed numbers) by replacing given fractions with equivalent fractions in such a way as to produce an equivalent sum or difference of fractions with like denominators. *For example, 2/3 + 5/4 = 8/12 + 15/12 = 23/12. (In general, a/b + c/d = (ad + bc)/bd.)*

CCSS.MATH.CONTENT.5.NF.A.2 Solve word problems involving addition and subtraction of fractions referring to the same whole, including cases of unlike denominators, e.g., by using visual fraction models or equations to represent the problem. Use benchmark fractions and number sense of fractions to estimate mentally and assess the reasonableness of answers. *For example, recognize an incorrect result 2/5 + 1/2 = 3/7, by observing that 3/7 < 1/2.*

Apply and extend previous understandings of multiplication and division

CCSS.MATH.CONTENT.5.NF.B.3 Interpret a fraction as division of the numerator by the denominator (*a/b = a ÷ b*). Solve word problems involving division of whole numbers leading to answers in the form of fractions or mixed numbers, e.g., by using visual fraction models or equations to represent the problem. *For example, interpret 3/4 as the result of dividing 3 by 4, noting that 3/4 multiplied by 4 equals 3, and that when 3 wholes are shared equally among 4 people each person has a share of size 3/4. If 9 people want to share a 50-pound sack of rice equally by weight, how many pounds of rice should each person get? Between what two whole numbers does your answer lie?*

CCSS.MATH.CONTENT.5.NF.B.4 Apply and extend previous understandings of multiplication to multiply a fraction or whole number by a fraction.

CCSS.MATH.CONTENT.5.NF.B.4.A

Interpret the product (*a/b*) × *q* as *a* parts of a partition of *q* into *b* equal parts; equivalently, as the result of a sequence of operations *a* × *q* ÷ *b*. *For example, use a visual fraction model to show (2/3) × 4 = 8/3, and create a story context for this equation. Do the same with (2/3) × (4/5) = 8/15. (In general, (a/b) × (c/d) = ac/bd.)*

CCSS.MATH.CONTENT.5.NF.B.4.B

Find the area of a rectangle with fractional side lengths by tiling it with unit squares of the appropriate unit fraction side lengths, and show that the area is the same as would be found by multiplying the side lengths. Multiply fractional side lengths to find areas of rectangles, and represent fraction products as rectangular areas.

CCSS.MATH.CONTENT.5.NF.B.5 Interpret multiplication as scaling (resizing), by:

CCSS.MATH.CONTENT.5.NF.B.5.A

Comparing the size of a product to the size of one factor on the basis of the size of the other factor, without performing the indicated multiplication.

CCSS.MATH.CONTENT.5.NF.B.5.B

Explaining why multiplying a given number by a fraction greater than 1 results in a product greater than the given number (recognizing multiplication by whole numbers greater than 1 as a familiar case); explaining why multiplying a given number by a fraction less than 1 results in a product smaller than the given number; and relating the principle of fraction equivalence *a/b = (n × a)/(n × b)* to the effect of multiplying *a/b* by 1.

CCSS.MATH.CONTENT.5.NF.B.6 Solve real world problems involving multiplication of fractions and mixed numbers, e.g., by using visual fraction models or equations to represent the problem.